CONTENTS

Vi James, family carer, tries out a Reminiscence drawing exercise with Madeline Armstrong, project worker. (London)

'REMEMBERING YESTERDAY, CARING TODAY'

This publication has arisen from the work of the above international Reminiscence Project, run by the European Reminiscence Network which involved reminiscence with people with dementia and their family carers.

CO-ORDINATION
Pam Schweitzer (UK)

CONSULTANTS
Faith Gibson (UK)
Nori Graham (UK)

EVALUATORS
Errollyn Bruce and
Faith Gibson (UK)

Marianne Heinemann-Knoch
and Birgit Jansen (Germany)

**NETWORK PARTNERS,
PROJECT LEADERS AND
GROUP WORKERS**

AUSTRIA

Vienna
Brigitte Habres
Heinrich Hoffer
Doris Otte

Salzburg
Monika Geck
Karin Rumpold
Maria Schrötzhammer
Sissi Weinbacker

Amstetten
Gerlin Schreier
Maria Schuller

BELGIUM

Brussels
Marie-Louise Carrette,
Edith Engelart
Cecile Fransen
Catherine Goor

Leuven:
Dirk Doucet

DENMARK
Ove Dahl
Marianne Kjer
Brita Lovendahl

FINLAND
Jonquil Cartlidge
Taina Johansson

FRANCE
Wandelo Beck
Arlette Goldberg

GERMANY

Kassel
Angelika Trilling
Diane Heine

Kircheim/Teck
Irene Hummel
Inge Fischer,
Brigitte Reich

Geislingen
Sonja Häberle
Irene Hummel
Heike Scherny-Hartkorn

THE NETHERLANDS
Pauline Bindel
Pollo Hamburger
Louise Meijer
Marita van Onna

NORWAY
Liv Hulteng
Lise Naess
Bengt-Ole Nordstroem

SWEDEN
Eva-Lena Gustafsson
Lotta Isacs
Anne Sandhölm
Annelie Sjörström

UNITED KINGDOM

London
Madeline Armstrong
Margaret Heath
Pam Schweitzer
Hannah Zeilig

Bradford
Errollyn Bruce
Mark Haslam
Sarah Hodgson

Members of the European Reminiscence Network at a training session in London, 1998

REMINISCING WITH PEOPLE WITH DEMENTIA

A Handbook for Carers

written by Errollyn Bruce, Sarah Hodgson & Pam Schweitzer

Photographs by Alex Schweitzer, Rado Klose and many others

Published by Age Exchange
for the European Reminiscence Network

© Age Exchange Theatre Trust, November 1999
The Reminiscence Centre, 11 Blackheath Village,
London SE3 9LA
Tel. ++44 20 8318 9105
Fax ++44 20 8318 0060
e-mail: age-exchange@lewisham.gov.uk
www.age-exchange.org.uk

Design & production: Learning Design, London

i

PREFACE

'Remembering Yesterday, Caring Today' is designed to help professional and family carers to improve communication with their people with dementia. It shows how carers can build on their remaining abilities, especially their capacity to remember the distant past, their intact social skills and their willingness to respond positively when they find themselves in an encouraging and accepting environment.

As well as providing many ideas for carers to use on a one-to-one basis and at home, the writers offer a wealth of imaginative activities to try out in groups, whether these take place in the community, in day centres, in residential settings or in local Alzheimers Disease Societies. What is especially innovative is the "Remembering Yesterday, Caring Today" approach of working with mixed groups of family carers and people with dementia with a view to reinforcing their relationship at a time when it is almost certainly undergoing severe strain.

Having fun together and valuing what remains are the key ideas underlying Remembering Yesterday, Caring Today Project, and as a result, this book makes refreshing and encouraging reading for all those who find themselves caring for people with dementia.

Early memories are precious to all of us. Most of us, though, have a continuous stream of memories from childhood to the present time. For the person with dementia, these early childhood memories are not just precious, they are often the only thread they have to make contact with their own identity. Helping the person with dementia recapture their early memories is one of the most rewarding tasks that carers can accomplish.

This manual will give a new impetus to carers who are looking for positive ways to engage with those they care for.

Nori Graham.

Dr Nori Graham, Chairman, Alzheimers Disease International

Mr. Zurburg tells the rest of the group how he used to play with a wooden spinning top when he was a child. (Amsterdam)

FOREWORD

This manual is a rich reservoir of ideas and practical suggestions about how to use reminiscence to enrich communication with people with dementia and to enhance relationships between them and their carers. It outlines an innovatory approach to supporting carers by emphasising mutual engagement in the present. By drawing on long established memories of the past it demonstrates how to involve people with dementia, their professional and especially their family carers in stimulating pleasurable, sociable activities.

At the same time, this manual manages to be intensely practical as well as being visionary and inspirational. This is because it is founded on the actual experience of an innovatory ten country European Commission funded project, 'Remembering Yesterday, Caring Today' in which new ideas about carer support and training in reminiscence were pioneered. Without minimising the difficulties, it shows how it is possible to involve many people with dementia and their carers in a wide variety of enjoyable activities which celebrate shared lives and make it possible for them to enjoy each other's company in the present.

The manual illustrates how to use planned reminiscence activities within sociable groups and then to continue to apply these ideas in stimulating people at home. It shows how necessary it is to enable carers to engage in their own reminiscing processes and to appreciate the potential of reminiscence as a vehicle for communicating with others. It emphasises how to create regular opportunities for socialising in congenial groups in the company of accepting people - other carers and people with dementia, arts workers and health and social care professionals. It shows how carers can learn from each other, how people with dementia are able to utilise their rusty social skills and how professionals can, with creativity and imagination, extend their conventional ideas and approaches.

Transcending national boundaries, the ideas clearly described and richly illustrated in this manual can be taken and readily adapted according to each country and practice context. I welcome this very practical addition to the international reminiscence literature and congratulate the European Reminiscence Network on its production.

My hope is that it will be widely read and energetically used to inform person-centred communication with people with dementia and to support family and other carers in the onerous demands which dementia care makes upon them.

Faith Gibson,
Emeritus Professor of Social Work,
University of Ulster, Northern Ireland

Sharing photos and memories in a relaxed atmosphere (Kassel)

INTRODUCTION

This manual is intended for people wishing to bring something special into the lives of people with dementia. People with dementia often have the ability to recall long-term, deeply rooted personal memories when the details of recent events escape them. Reminiscence uses this ability. Memories are sparked by hearing other people sharing their own personal stories about their lives.

Where this sharing of past experience takes place in a friendly and relaxed group situation, the person with dementia can rediscover a sense of identity, of fun and of belonging which can last for some considerable time beyond the activity itself. Revisiting key parts of life can help those who are disoriented to rebuild a sense of the continuity between past and present and to hold on more firmly to a positive sense of self.

Participating in this process can be very rewarding for carers, especially those who are in a long-term relationship with the person with dementia, as it strengthens the bonds between them and reminds them of the good times they have shared over the years.

The manual is a tool kit for people wishing to try out reminiscence as a way to reach out to and connect with people who have dementia. It is the result of a successful European experiment, Remembering Yesterday, Caring Today (or RYCT as it came to be called) in which project leaders in ten countries set up pilot groups of people with dementia, family carers and volunteers. The purpose was to try out the effectiveness of reminiscence as a way of enjoying time together and supporting one another through the experience of an extremely testing illness.

In 16 groups across Europe, leaders followed the same project outline of reminiscence training and

Carol, a volunteer, is enjoying a story told by Edith, aged 90. (London)

3

activities. They recorded what worked well, what needed re-thinking and what new ideas emerged during the running of the project. The most successful ideas have been gathered together in this manual.

We begin by explaining the thinking behind the project - a positive attitude to the problems of living with dementia, creative exploration of reminiscence, a person-centred approach, and how these can be combined in practice.

We then offer a wide range of practical ideas and exercises for exploring themes common to all our lives - childhood, schooldays, working life and adult home life. This exploration can take place in a group, or outside it, in the home environment or in the community. Activities can be tailored to a wide range of situations and the idea is that participants make reminiscence part of daily life.

Readers may be working with groups of people with dementia (and sometimes their family carers) in a wide variety of settings, such as hospitals, support groups, day centres, care homes or community groups. Some may be working with people with dementia in their own homes. We refer in the manual to group leaders, volunteers, people with dementia and family carers, but we anticipate that readers will adapt our ideas and format to suit their own situations, and will pick themes and activities which reflect the needs and interests of their participants.

MAP OF EUROPE SHOWING WHERE 'REMEMBERING YESTERDAY, CARING TODAY' PROJECTS WERE BASED

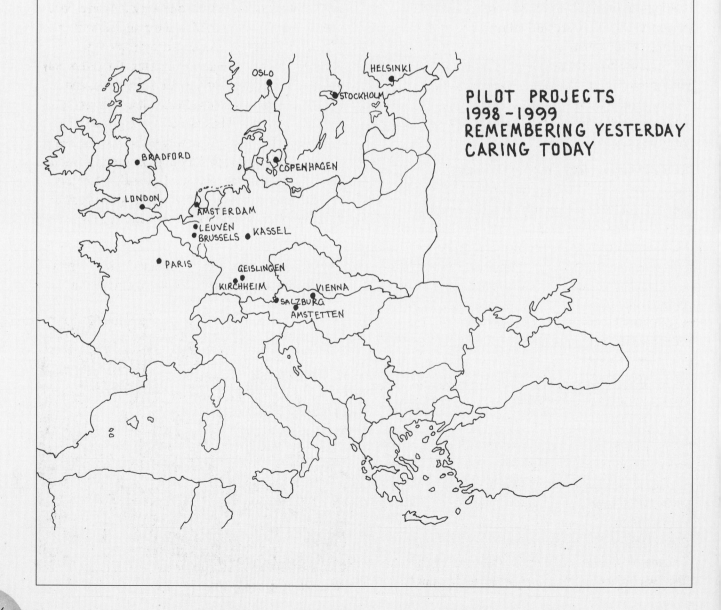

PILOT PROJECTS
1998 - 1999
REMEMBERING YESTERDAY
CARING TODAY

The Remembering Yesterday, Caring Today Project

RYCT used reminiscence with people with dementia and their family or other carers. It aimed to teach carers the basics of reminiscence work, good listening skills, being non-judgemental and reacting sensitively to efforts to communicate. It introduced carers to the idea that spending time listening to the person they care for, and enjoying the memories that remain, can be like a tonic, helping the person with dementia feel better and more confident. By reminiscing themselves, carers were able to appreciate the enjoyment and social benefits of talking about their own past with others. They became comfortable with using reminiscence as a strategy for improving daily life for themselves and the person they are caring for. It offered a way of making the most of the relationship with their person as they now are and stimulating positive feelings, while giving them space to grieve for the old relationship that they have lost. By establishing joint groups of people with dementia and their carers, it helped carers to relax, feel at ease and make supportive friendships in a social situation with the person they care for.

The RYCT projects in the different countries aimed to recruit participants relatively early in the course of their illness. Some had only recently been diagnosed, and some had been coping for some years without accessing services such as day care, respite care or seeking support from voluntary organisations working with dementia. Some of these carers had not come into contact with others in a similar position and needed the opportunity to share experiences. Time was set aside therefore in the first weeks of the project for this to happen. However it was emphasised from the start that the project was not primarily a carers' support group and carers were encouraged to join other local groups or organisations for this type of help.

The projects began with several meetings for group leaders, helpers and volunteers. These meetings introduced members of the team to each other and allowed information about dementia, reminiscence and the aims of the project to be shared and discussed. The team members then recruited families who wished to participate in the project. This involved visiting them in their own homes and describing to them the aims,

methods and duration of the project. It also gave the team members an opportunity to build up a sense of the family's situation and background.

Four initial project meetings then followed. These acted as induction or training meetings for the carers and the volunteers *(see section on page 51 on early meetings)*. Carers practised reminiscence activities and in the process everyone got to know one another. In some projects, where carers were reluctant or unable to leave their person elsewhere, those they cared for also attended these early meetings but met in a separate room with other project workers and volunteers, and their resulting higher degree of involvement in the project proved beneficial.

Following these initial meetings, a pattern of alternate sessions was established. On one week the carers met, evaluated the previous session and planned the next one. The following week carers and people with dementia met and reminisced together. The carers-only sessions allowed time for the carers' memories and feelings to be heard, so that in the joint sessions, maximum time could be devoted to the people with dementia. Where the people with dementia had their own sessions running parallel with the carers' sessions, they were able to make relationships with volunteers, and they in turn were able to give helpful feedback to the carers about what their people had remembered and recognised.

The RYCT project has provided a model which is now being further explored and developed throughout

Remembering happy times (Kassel)

Europe and can be adapted to suit local needs and resources. The project was developed for working with people in groups, but it can be applied to very small groups, for example, the person with dementia, a carer and a befriender or reminiscence worker. Although readers may not want, or be able, to follow the RYCT format, this manual emphasises the particular value of providing a space where carers and people with dementia can enjoy themselves together. There are few places where this may happen and the RYCT project workers in all the countries concerned found that the combination of reminiscence and providing a normal and enjoyable social occasion gave a real boost to both carers and those they care for.

The Essential Features of the RYCT Approach

The RYCT approach aims to help people with dementia to make relationships and to communicate through reminiscence, in ways which take account of their current level of disability. By giving them the extra time, reassurance and encouragement that many of them need to be able to join in, and reserving a space at the centre of things for them, it gives them the experience of being valued members of a desirable social group. RYCT uses the 'group effect' to stimulate people with dementia to do things they would not be inspired to do elsewhere, providing opportunities for creative expression in a failure-free environment and creating moments of celebration and mutual appreciation.

The RYCT approach increases confidence and builds on people's remaining skills. It does this by listening to everyone's stories attentively and non-judgmentally, and accepting contributions which

may stray from the stated reminiscence theme of the day. It recognises that it is inappropriate to correct people with dementia or undermine the 'truth' of their accounts. Every individual will have their own memories of events and situations and these memories are 'true' for them. The feelings they express and the efforts they make to communicate are valuable in themselves.

"In the telling and retelling, the detail of a memory alters somewhat. Both the context and the interaction between the teller and the listener influence the story. It does not matter if the details change.

Think of it more as a picture being painted and repainted in changing light.

While the major characteristics or core remains recognisable, the details alter, reflecting differences of emphasis, mood, memory and interpretation."

Faith Gibson in 'Reminiscence and Recall', page 14

Now in dementia this process can go many stages further - the core may not remain recognisable, the details can disappear, take over all together or be amalgamated with details from other experiences. A story may be a metaphorical way to talk about present experience, it may make no sense literally but have symbolic meaning.

Carers develop their listening skills, sometimes working with their own person and sometimes with another (Kassel)

A Positive Approach to Dementia

Understanding Dementia

There is a tendency to think of dementia as a disaster - a personality destroying disorder about which nothing effective can be done. This view is not helpful to people who are living with the condition. Dementia is a term used to describe a decline in a person's mental powers, particularly memory. It tells us that a person is experiencing persistent mental decline that is presumed to be caused by changes in their brain. There are a number of different brain problems that lead to dementia, the two most common being vascular dementia and Alzheimer's Disease. It is important to remember that diagnosis of the underlying causes is not easy.

Dementia usually involves loss of memory along with one or more other mental functions (for example comprehension, judgement, planning); these losses affect people's ability to perform daily tasks and organise their lives in a wide variety of different ways. A more helpful view than the disaster one sees dementia as resulting in a number of disabilities, and emphasises the huge variation between different people's patterns of impairment and decline. A sympathetic physical and social environment can reduce the impact of disabilities, and people can be helped to maintain quality of life, albeit a different kind of life to the one they led before.

Nellie is someone who has always enjoyed being in the limelight. Although now very disabled and not able to communicate easily, she blossoms when given special attention by other members of the group. (Bradford)

Having dementia means that there will be a number of things that people cannot do without help. In addition they will have feelings about what is happening to them (for example frustration, grief, anger) which may lead to behaviour that other people mistakenly dismiss as part of their illness, and therefore something about which nothing can be done.

And most important, other people tend to treat people with dementia differently, treatment that can add up to the message 'you are now unimportant, damaged and no longer playing a full part in your social world'. We cannot remove the underlying problems that give rise to their disabilities, but we can help people with their feelings about what is happening, and respond to them in ways which make them feel valued and important as people.Reminiscence work is one way to give this kind of help.

To sum up, to do the best for people who have dementia, we need to look at each individual, notice their own particular disabilities and work out how best they can be supported in their lives.

A reminiscence project can provide opportunities for showing love and care. (Kassel)

We need to assume that there is meaning in what they do and say and learn ways of interpreting imaginatively so that like detectives we can 'crack the code'. We also need to develop our ability to work at the level of the heart, as well as the head. There is often coherence at the feeling level, and by empathising we can enter and share their world, to some extent at least.

The word 'Dementia'

Many people with dementia have never been told what is wrong with them and families vary widely when it comes to how comfortable they feel about using the various diagnostic labels. We need to discover what words the people we work with are comfortable with. If people think of their problems as stroke damage, or memory loss, we can use their words. In fact it is useful to be precise about the specific disabilities people have and talk about these openly, without recourse to medical terms. It can be more helpful to say *"When your brain isn't connecting things together properly..."* or *"When the things you see don't look the same as they used to.."* rather than *"When you've got Alzheimer's..."* For some people, the medical terms may have terrible associations.

A man whose wife had Alzheimer's disease said,

"I wish they wouldn't call it a disease. For me that word is connected with horrible things like filth, chaos, war and poverty, and her life isn't like that at all."

Carer, Bradford

"One daughter in my group suffered very much from her mother's disorientation and needed to protect herself. The word dementia was never used. Instead we spoke of memory difficulties."

Arlette Goldberg, Parls

Thinking about the experiences of people who have dementia

To communicate with people with dementia we need to tune in to how they are experiencing life. We need to understand the difficulties that different people with dementia are having and how they are feeling, and find ways to reduce the impact of their difficulties and to put them at their ease.

People with dementia often feel they are misunderstood. They have usually experienced:

● other people taking over, speaking for them, looking bored, embarrassed or puzzled when they are talking

● people patronising them, 'talking down' to them or bossing them about

● people talking about them in front of them, and ignoring them if they have something to say

● people being angry with them, blaming them for actions which arise from their inability to understand situations and assuming them to be making things difficult on purpose

● people dismissing something that is very real and important to them as silly people doing and saying things for them that they can say or do themselves if given time.

People with dementia do not experience the world in the same way as they used to. Feelings of anxiety and insecurity mean that they often:

● find new situations daunting

● need to stay close to their carer to feel safe and secure

● feel anxious about things that are very real to them (but incomprehensible or insignificant to others)

● need reassurance about what is happening, often repeating questions about what is going on

● retreat into memories with which they feel secure, often repeating stories.

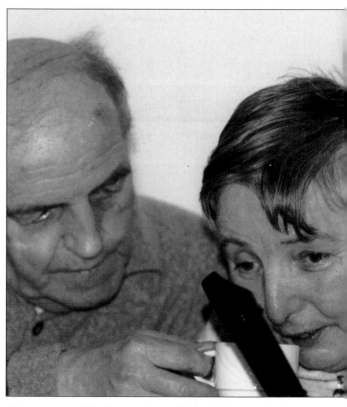

The person with dementia needs and deserves support, understanding and the company of others. (Kassel)

Changes in their ability to understand events mean that they may:

● find that things look strange and not 'right' in some way; for many people the strangeness feels menacing and unpredictable

● receive incomplete or distorted information from their senses and/or from their memory stores

● fail to access the memories of past experience which help them to make sense of what is happening in the here and now

● cannot reliably tell the difference between reality and fantasy

● cannot bring to awareness the vital detail which makes sense of a situation

● rely to a large extent on cues in the here and now to work out what is going on (e.g. if we greet them like a friend, they often assume that we are a friend)

● are unable to select the most relevant features from all the information their senses are providing.

The process of communication inevitably changes. They may:

● know what they want to say, but find that the words won't come out

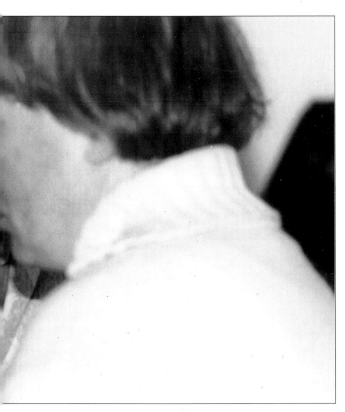

● lose track of what they want to do or say half way along

● experience difficulties in finding the right word or using words in the correct order

● be slow to switch on to what is happening, find it hard to keep their attention and lose concentration, thereby getting left behind in conversation.

Like anyone else, people with dementia have the capacity to feel sad, happy, embarrassed, humiliated, elated, shamed, but are less able to cope with their feelings. They may:

● experience things very intensely

● be very tuned in to the body language and feelings of others

● become less inhibited about showing their feelings, needs and wants

● rely on their senses in new ways, for example enjoying physical contact, responding to music.

As a result of having dementia, people have to cope with feeling less in control of life than before. They often:

● make mistakes, and find different ways to cope with this unpleasant experience

● make attempts to 'cover' their mistakes, for example, pretending to understand when they don't

● feel bored and dissatisfied and are unable to find things to do without help and support from others (both to get going and to keep going)

For many, developing dementia leads to reduced social confidence and withdrawal from many social situations. Becoming part of a reminiscence group or project is a way of making new contacts and restoring sociability.

We can use reminiscence as a way to remind people of past feelings of self-esteem, confidence and competence. By valuing their memories from the past, we show them that they are valued in the present.

Thinking about the experiences of family carers

Family carers develop an understanding of dementia from their own experience, from professionals and from other sources. The printed information they receive can be overwhelming and very threatening. Books and leaflets tend to describe all the different things that can go wrong and imply a misleading level of certainty.

For example, *"Alzheimer's Disease is a progressive and terminal illness"* sounds terrible. It does not tell us that many people with AD have long periods without noticeable decline, live for many years after their symptoms appear and die of other causes.

If carers develop a *'disaster'* view of dementia it may be harder for them to come to terms with their person's present state, and it can also influence the kind of care that they give. The *'disability'* view of dementia is more hopeful and suggests that much can be done to improve the quality of life of a person who has dementia and to help them adjust to, and make the most of, their remaining abilities.

> ❝*A daughter who felt that her mother was never in tune with her needs as a child had great difficulty recognising her mother's needs when she developed dementia and tended to assume that she was deliberately making life difficult.*
>
> *The mother's forgetfulness and inability to think clearly meant that she was incapable of devious plans, but her daughter found this hard to believe.*
>
> *Despite this, she was still visiting her mother on a daily basis.*❞

Bradford

To do good work with carers we need to understand how they are experiencing the situation. Some people find themselves caring because of co-residence, but the vast majority of informal carers are people with a long-standing relationship of attachment to the person they care for. The majority are spouses/partners or children. Some may have had a difficult relationship with the

Rose, born in Budapest, is sitting beside her youngest son Armand, his wife and their daughter. They all participated in the project and were delighted to hear their mother's memories, many of them for the first time. (Paris)

person they care for, and this past relationship is bound to have a bearing on the level of stress in the present, but there is no reason to assume that the bond is any less strong.

The onset of dementia brings feelings of grief. The person is no longer as they were, and the carer experiences many losses. At the same time, unlike someone who has been bereaved by death, the carer is having to adapt the old relationship to deal with the person as they now are - very much alive and needing more from them than ever before. Spouse carers in

Life has become more stressful for Jim and Vi since he developed memory difficulties. Involvement in the RYCT reminiscence project allows them to enjoy shared memories of their earlier days together for the first time in a long while. (London)

particular tend to find that they share the contracting social world of the person they care for as dependency increases. Carers may have a great need to express these feelings of grief and frustration and to talk about the problems of caring.

All carers need to re-work the relationship with the person they care for and let go of old expectations that are now unrealistic (e.g. *"He always used to lock the back door at night, but now he forgets."*) Some carers are flexible and easily adjust their expectations and responses, others find this very difficult. In particular, carers need to learn to change established ways of communicating to accommodate their person's difficulties.

"A carer who was exhausted but full of good will at the beginning of the RYCT project would tell her husband off and correct him every time he made a mistake.

This was an attempt to keep him 'normal' rather than admitting his disabilities. By the end of the project, she felt good about being able to accept him in his present state.

She had gained knowledge and understanding of dementia and its symptoms. Her anguish and anger had been reduced and, as a result, the pressure she put on him was lessened."

Brussels

Family carers often hope for miracle cures and may half-hope for unrealistically great things from a reminiscence project. Compared with what they are really wanting - their person restored to their former level of mental competence - the small gains of a reminiscence group or project may seem insignificant.

However some carers are heartened to see the people enjoying themselves and to see unexpected abilities or memories emerge. They may discover new ways to live life alongside a person with dementia that make it more rewarding.

Remembering Yesterday - Caring Today

Remembering yesterday, caring today,
That says it all in a new kind of way.
For remembering has given so much to me,
Reassurance, a direction, greater sensibility.
I now have another challenge in my life,
Not only being a loving, caring wife.
I never thought I could feel this way,
I'm thinking of things I just have to say.
Putting it in verse, I would never have dreamt,
So thanks to the project,
Every word I say is meant.

My husband's needs must come first now,
For in sickness and in health I took a vow,
I will come to terms with this illness,
Even though I still don't know how.
The project has taught me so many things,
To have patience and think of others' feelings.
Get down to their level when sitting in a chair,
Hold hands, say your name,
to let them know who's there.
Speak softly and slowly, never ever shout,
Don't reprimand:
They don't know what they're about.

Our tête-à-têtes are now in the past,
But you do give me signs that I understand.
The special look, with that cheeky smile,
And a warm squeeze of the hand.

The love we have together,
Will be with us till we part,
Till my strength gives up on me,
I'll be there, sweetheart.

The above is a poem written by Joan Sharp, a family carer in the London project who has found that writing poetry is a way of coming to terms with her husband's dementia.

At the first session, Joan was asked to write down her hopes for the project and this is what she said:

"My hopes are to make friends with others in the same situation as myself, to gain knowledge of what to expect as my husband's illness progresses. I hope I can help Jim recapture some of the happy times we have spent together, also with his family and friends."

The experience of others working with or caring for people with dementia

Professional carers working with people with dementia (for example in day centres or residential care or as paid carers in the person's home) often find that they are looking after a person about whom they know very little. They see the person as they are now, and find it difficult to imagine what they were like when they were younger, more active and healthy.

> *It is as though workers in the field of ageing are observers in the arena at the end of a Marathon race where they see people coming in for the last lap, tired and weary.*
>
> *They only see them tired and weary and rarely enquire how these old people have run the race. I have always been interested in how people have run the race because that tells us why they are tired and weary and it reveals a lot about how we might refresh them, because we learn so much about their vitality, their tenacity, their intelligence, their capability, which are not always evident when tiredness and weariness are the manifest symptoms.*

Professor Malcolm Johnson, University of Bristol, taken from Reminiscence Magazine, Issue 9, October 1994..

Lack of knowledge about the past of a person with dementia makes it much more difficult to provide them with the most appropriate stimulus or to interpret successfully their efforts at communication. Many such efforts can be dismissed as mere attention-seeking, or even as destructive behaviour, if important signals and cues are not understood by the carer. With few genuinely satisfying interactions, the process of looking after a person with dementia can be very frustrating and can lead to the carer finding it difficult to see the person behind the disability.

Setting aside some time to find out about a person's past life and interests can be very difficult in the face of busy working schedules and staff shortages. However, making time to do this will have many benefits for both the people with dementia and members of staff.

> *People with dementia's memories are like a landscape where only the mountain tops now remain.*

Group leader speaking to carers, Copenhagen

Finding out about the important life experiences of a person with dementia can also be very difficult if that person is already very disabled and finds it hard to remember and communicate for themselves. Often the only facts available are on the patient's medical records or admission forms, but these are often more about the physical condition of the person, rather than about their past or present social situation. If these notes can be amplified with biographical information and details about the person's family, working life, likes, dislikes, and their past special interests, a more rounded picture can emerge and opportunities can be provided for more positive and more personal interactions with staff and other clients.

Staff from Flevohuis Residential Home and Day Centre, visit a local museum with clients and their family carers. (Amsterdam)

Reminiscence: what is it and is it a worthwhile activity?

Reminiscence is thinking or talking about one's life experience in order to share memories and reflect on the past. The activity can be conducted formally by a group leader as part of a structured activity in a residential or community setting, or informally between friends or family. There are many types of reminiscence and many reasons for doing it, but in this manual the emphasis is on using reminiscence as a way of encouraging and supporting social interaction and enjoyment.

Reminiscing is a natural part of most people's lives and is a pleasurable social activity. It is a means of making links with others through sharing past experiences and reflecting together on the present. Older people often enjoy taking stock of their past lives, especially in the company of old friends. However, where partners and contemporaries have died or moved away, social gatherings with remaining contacts can be difficult to organise, as mobility, distance or other difficulties get in the way. For these people, a more structured reminiscence group can be an enjoyable way of making new friends and offering mutual support and understanding.

Because the content of reminiscence is personal and particular, it serves as a fast track to knowing and appreciating the other people involved. When we reminisce we reveal small, but significant details about our lives which are not normally shared early on in a relationship. The combining of many people's specific memories creates a community of experience, in which everybody feels they have a stake. The newly shared experiences and memories form a basis on which the group can then participate in social and cultural activities with highly therapeutic results.

This can boost the confidence of the individuals involved so that they become more bold and experimental in what they will attempt. This is particularly the case where the reminiscence activities go beyond talking about the past and move into creative explorations of memories through writing, drama, movement and music. These explorations, which may or may not result in tangible end products, make the life experience of the participants more visible and accessible to both others and themselves. They are also memorable events in themselves and help to confirm the life and the shared history of the group.

Eileen is an old friend of Jim's and she attends the sessions as a volunteer so that her memories of past time together can help him to retrieve his own. (London)

Revisiting shared memories can bring couples closer together at a time when their relationship may be under particular stress. (Copenhagen)

There will be some people for whom the idea of reminiscing will be difficult, perhaps because they have unhappy or painful memories, or because they are worried about revealing themselves to people they do not know very well. Some may not want to join a group as a result of these feelings, while others may listen rather than talk, until they know members of the group better. In any group it is very likely that painful as well as happy memories will be shared as trust builds up and close relationships are made. In a well-established group this is quite normal and group members will be able to support each other whatever feelings emerge.

For staff and volunteers working with older people in day centres, hospitals and homes, doing reminiscence work is a means of individualising the clients, acknowledging the breadth of their past experience and getting to know them better. Where family carers can be contacted and are willing to be involved, they can help to fill in the gaps and provide information about important people and events in their person's

life. This can be a positive experience for them as it gives them a continuing role to play, even though they are no longer the sole or main carer. Of course there may be a huge difference between the story as told by the person with dementia and by the carer, and both need to be respected. Many studies have shown that staff who have knowledge of the life histories of the people in their care treat them with more respect and sensitivity. They often find their own work more rewarding and meaningful as a result of their closer ties and greater understanding.

For family carers, reminiscence can be a way of staying in touch with the past lives which they and the person they care for have shared. Drawing on past positive experiences can help both the carer and the person with dementia to cope better with present difficulties. If carers can weave reminiscence into the daily lives of their person, they can find it a valuable way to stimulate good feelings and make the daily routine run more smoothly. Reminiscence can slot into and enhance established and effective coping strategies.

Reminiscence Work Skills

Although skills are needed to do reminiscence work no formal qualification is required. Anyone who enjoys the company of other people and likes hearing stories can acquire the necessary skills. Those needed for effective reminiscence work include the ability to:

● listen attentively

● retain what you have heard and make connections

● empathise
(understand how the other person is feeling)

● relate to other people in a sensitive way

● cope with the expression of painful emotions

● demonstrate an interest in the past.

Although the same skills, sensitivity, tact and the ability to listen, are needed when working with people with dementia, they need additional help to enable them to retrieve and fully enjoy the memories they have. A wider range of approaches must be developed in order to tap into every kind of communication still available to the person with dementia. This might include stimulating all their senses and responding positively to verbal and non-verbal attempts to communicate.

Pat, a family carer, listens to Gertie, a member of the reminiscence group, and draws out her memories.

Reasons for reminiscing with people with Dementia

Reminiscence is a pleasurable experience both for the listener and the person who is reminiscing.

● It focuses on early memories, which often remain very strong after the ability to remember more recent events deteriorates.

Lisa Naess, group leader, Norway, using reminiscence as an engaging way of getting to know other people in the present by sharing experience of the past. (Oslo)

● It allows people with dementia to go back to a time when they were active and healthy and re-experience how they felt then, for example feeling confident and in control, compared with the present.

● It gives a degree of control to people with dementia. They decide what memories to reveal and how much they *'trust'* the person they are talking to with their memories.

● It allows the person who is listening to learn more about the person with dementia's past. This can help in understanding the present behaviour and feelings of the person they are caring for.

● It provides a framework of activity which can be used and enjoyed on a daily basis. As the person becomes more disabled, it can be difficult to find things to do.

● People with dementia, and their carers, often find that going out in public can be difficult. Friends and family may find the disability awkward and stay away because of this. A reminiscence group allows people with dementia and their carers to get to know others in a social setting. It expands their social world.

● Recording memories, key figures and important dates in the life of a person with dementia's life and making a life history can help later when that person becomes more disabled and can no longer remember or communicate these things for themselves.

● If or when the person with dementia goes into residential care, a life history or other form of tangible reminiscence record helps staff to get to know and understand that person as an individual.

Developing friendship and understanding in a reminiscence group (Kassel)

Reminiscence as Communication

A family carer listens with full attention. (Copenhagen)

Reminiscence is about communication and we need to think about how to communicate effectively with people with dementia. When talking to some people with dementia who may find it difficult to understand what we are saying and meaning at times, we need to:

- find different ways of saying the same thing to make sure it is understood

- use simple language and say one thing at a time

- use accompanying gestures to help convey the meaning of what is being said

- allow time for ideas and information to be digested

- watch for signs that the person has understood and interpret their signals with imagination and creativity

- help the person to connect with others in the group by noticing and pointing out links and similarities.

"People suffering from dementia are often called communication handicapped because they cannot find the right words. But such a person may well have something which he or she wants to communicate. That is why it is so important to listen actively to the person with dementia, especially to the feelings, and try to understand what it is he or she is trying to communicate.

Listening demands commitment, presence and a willingness to identify with the other person's problems. To listen actively is to express interest in the other person, to recognise the importance of their feelings and respect them."

Brita Lovendahl, Copenhagen

Being able to listen and give our full attention is especially important when working with people with dementia. We need to work hard to ensure that the person with dementia is relaxed and feels valued and accepted. To achieve this we need to:

- give full attention and show we are interested

- use body language which conveys our attention - for example nodding, sitting forwards, making eye contact

- sit at the same level as the person with dementia

- respect their space and do not 'crowd' them, but make physical contact if this feels appropriate and welcome.

- respect and accept what is said - for example by not interrupting or challenging what the person is trying to communicate.

- allow silences to occur without feeling we have to fill them.

- remember what the person has said and reflect it back to them in ways which show we have understood and retained it.

- give the person time to express things in their own way and assume that there is meaning in what they are saying or communicating

- respond warmly to what they have to say

- acknowledge the 'feeling content' of what is being said, rather than focusing only on the surface meaning.

"When I am working with people with dementia, I begin to make contact with the person by total concentration on relationship through words, tone of voice, eye contact, body language and touch - above all by listening to what they have to tell me and writing down, as best I can, what I hear. I do not practise detachment, I do not have an agenda, I do not have any prior knowledge of the person - I just try to be with them in their condition and share their concerns. The messages I bring back from the frontiers of communication seem to me often remarkable, moving and humbling."

John Killick, Writer in Residence, Westminster Healthcare.

MONKEY PUZZLE

A poem by John Killick

I'm suffering from the Monkey Puzzle.
The Monkey Puzzle is this place.
The Puzzle is: how to cope with the
Monkeys.

I can't remember anything of today
except the peppering of my tongue. Yes,
my mouth was peppered again this
morning.
I believe it is part of the Monkey Puzzle.
These little Monkeys have two legs,
you know, and wear suits.

These whiskers that are growing
around the lower part of my face,
I did think they formed a part
of the category of the Monkey Puzzle,
put there to irritate newcomers.

I've come to the conclusion
that what we should do
is educate these Monkeys.
We should make it perfectly clear
that there are certain things
that are not done, even though
I know that they are laughing
their heads off behind my back.

People are pushing things down my neck.
I don't believe it's even for a joke -
it's pure badness. Next time anybody says
'Put that in your mouth!' I'll take a flying
leap and punch them.
It's an unignorable fact
that they are mucking me about.

If this is another bit of the Monkey Puzzle,
then Monkey will know what it's got!
I'll run amok a-shutter, I really will,
I'll just go wild and frighten them!

Because a person with dementia has memory difficulties, they can easily feel anxious about whether they will be able to remember.

To minimise this anxiety we need to:

● find ways of reminiscing with the person which avoid direct questioning

> **When looking at a wedding photograph, enjoy looking at it with the person with dementia, look at clothes and expressions, assume both of you are fresh to it.**
>
> **As you look together, facts and memories may come, but if you don't you will both have enjoyed the photograph and the person with dementia will not think they have failed.**
>
> **If you can find out before who the people in the photograph are, write the names in pencil on the back, and then if the person does not remember names you can both wonder who is in the photograph and turn the picture over to find out.**

● provide opportunities for the person to show recognition through nods and smiles without having to verbalise their reaction

"A carer did not ask his wife questions because her ability to speak had deteriorated. He told the story of the journeys they had made together and when she did not remember, he added details and showed photographs until she showed signs of recognition."

Amsterdam

● accompany the person with dementia, exploring objects and other triggers together, but without testing them about what the item was called or how it was used

● know as much as possible about the person with dementia's past, so that you can act as *'extra memory'* for them and help them draw on this past, connect with it, at relevant moments in the present

● Give the person with dementia plenty of time and encouragement, to allow them to reach the point where they are ready to speak for themselves.

"It was not until the fourth session that the people with dementia were ready to tell a story for themselves. By then they had become more confident, and were feeling relaxed and safe in the group."

Brussels

A person with dementia tells about a tapestry she made in the past. She is able to add in details as her memories are triggered (Amsterdam)

A friendly and convivial family atmosphere prevails in the specially appointed flat where the Belgian project took place. (Brussels)

● Be prepared to speak for the person if it will help them feel more relaxed and secure in a group.

> **One participant was very nervous every time she was going to tell her story. The pressure to speak was making her very anxious. So her husband said: "If you are so nervous, I will tell your story, and you nod your head to show that I am telling it right". She was much happier to come to meetings given this arrangement.**

Amsterdam

Atmosphere

People with dementia are often very sensitive to the atmosphere in a group and quick to pick up on other people's feelings, both positive and negative. Leaders and helpers need to set the tone in a group, signalling that this is a safe place to try things out without fear of failure.

It is important to have a culture of openness and humour about making mistakes. Leaders and helpers need to take risks themselves and let others laugh at them when things go wrong.

This helps people with dementia feel less self-conscious about their own mistakes. It is an antidote to the experience people with dementia may have of themselves as damaged, incompetent, losing control, in contrast with everyone else who may appear undamaged, competent, and in control. Leaders and helpers need to trust one another to be able to do this, and feel at ease with the people in the group who are not forgetful, and who will remember the silly things they have said and done.

> **One of the leaders came in to the meeting on the war years wearing a handkerchief with four knots in the corners, as women workers used to do in the past. The participants all thought this was hugely funny, laughing at how absurd she looked.**

Brussels

A party atmosphere, laughter, the sense of being somewhere where things happen, can act as a stimulus to people with dementia. Often they will do things in the group that they would never do elsewhere. If family carers are involved in a group doing reminiscence with the people they care for, they may need reassurance about this, as they can feel that they are failing if their person sinks into unresponsivity at home.

People with dementia need lots of support to awaken and sustain an interest in what is happening. Leaders and helpers need to be spread around the group, to give individual attention and help the people with dementia engage with what is going on.

Each person may need someone to draw their attention to things of interest, and to be ready to listen to their responses.

Group leaders must not expect too much and should be satisfied if some of the people with dementia are alert and happy in the group, but prefer to say nothing.

"One man smiled often but never spoke in the meetings. But in the day centre he never smiled. So for him, the group was a success."

Amsterdam

When doing reminiscence work with people with dementia considerable creativity may be needed to find ways to stimulate them to remember. The group leader has to make it worth their while to pay attention and to make the mental effort to remember.

They need to be feeling safe and secure to be able to think clearly. The right triggers need to be found to reach the memories that are still retrievable.

"Two participants had very little language left, but their body language expressed satisfaction and pleasure during the meetings. Very often we could observe them smiling and humming. Their wives told us that, when coming to our meeting place, they were very eager to get into the room, greeting everyone."

Oslo

Eileen helps Jim to join in an anniversary celebration during the project. (London)

The Use of Triggers in Reminiscence Work

A personal photograph can be a trigger for long-forgotten memories. (Brussels)

A trigger can be anything which evokes feelings or brings back memories. Although triggers are not always necessary in reminiscence, they are particularly valuable when working with people with dementia. Triggers can be objects, photographs, music, smells, tastes, textures, sounds and movement, in fact anything which stimulates the senses.

> **"One participant studied an atlas for some time, telling us that he had had one just the same at school. He was both delighted and enthusiastic over this discovery. We were pleased to hear such a long statement, as his wife told us that he seldom displayed initiative, and had great difficulty in expressing himself and putting a statement together."**
>
> **Group leader, Paris**

The abilities of participants must be considered when selecting triggers. For some who find it hard to hear and see clearly, it is important to provide opportunities for other senses to be stimulated. By providing a range of materials to feel, smell and taste, more members of the group can enjoy participating and relate to the theme.

When people have dementia, some types of memory may be less affected than others. Reminiscence work needs to tap into better preserved areas of memory, and these will be different for each individual. Some people will have good recall of events from their early life and be able to retrieve and share memories with others about this time. Some may retain good memory for actions when their ability to talk about those actions and their associations is lost. For others the sense of smell or touch, or the memory for sound, may be well preserved and may act as triggers to powerful feelings, even though they may not be able or wish to express these feelings in words.

Catherine Goor, group leader, starts a game of exploring objects just by their feel. (Brussels)

Some triggers are specific to certain groups of people. They may be culturally or regionally specific, or even vary from one town to another. Rhymes and street games for example will probably be remembered differently even by individuals who come from the same region. Some may be meaningful to women and others to men. Often the most powerful triggers are those that are specific to an individual person, a photograph or object which is special to them.

"Bluma had lived alone in her flat, but had become increasingly forgetful and unwell. After a fire in her apartment and an accident when she fell and broke her leg, she was placed in the residential home. She made no attempt to communicate with others and sat stiffly, not speaking or smiling, but staring straight ahead "like an Egyptian mummy".

Her son and daughter were desperately worried about her. Her son, who was visiting her from his home in Israel, begged me to do something to help her. I invited her daughter to bring her to the RYCT project group.

At the first session, the daughter brought along a samovar which had belonged to her grandmother. Her mother recognised it immediately, was very happy to see it, and began to relax. After four sessions, she began to speak. Now I sometimes see her sitting in the cafeteria (which is our socialising area) and speaking to other people there."

Group leader, Paris

Objects

Some objects will bring back memories for most people of a certain age, for example an old tin bath, or a scrubbing board. For people who were born in the early years of the twentieth century these will almost certainly be part of their childhood. Younger people will need different triggers, associated with their own earlier lives. Even where a trigger is *"age-appropriate"*, it may not work for a particular individual. You will need to explore and experiment to find what works for each member of your group.

"Marie was very reluctant to come to the sessions in the first place and worried about what she would have to do. I reassured her that she could just watch and listen and would not be asked anything. She would be free to speak only if and when she wanted to. She came and I asked her if she would like to sit next to me. Some objects were passed round.

Marie put a candlestick in her hand, a cabled one made from an olive tree, which was very old and originally came from Jerusalem. I asked her if she wanted to say something and she spoke very quietly. She remembered that her parents had one like this. This is the magic of the object as a mediator."

Group leader, Paris

An object may act as a trigger because of the way it looks and feels, as well as because of its associated memories. It will often have quite different associations for each member of the group.

"A tin containing buttons was enjoyed in a number of different ways. Edith used to make her own clothes and told the group about some of her favourite outfits.

Mary was delighted by the colour and the feel of the buttons and the sound they made in the tin. George was reminded (for some reason which we never found out) of treasure hunts he had been on as a young child. Nellie and a volunteer used the same buttons as counters in a game."

Bradford

It may be possible for groups or individuals to build up a collection of objects to use as triggers. They may be lent or given by family or friends or purchased from second-hand shops or car-boot sales.

Alternatively some local libraries, museums and voluntary organisations have handling collections which can be loaned out for reminiscence purposes.

Photographs

These can be personal, for example of the self or family or friends; they can be of places, for instance where a person grew up, or took holidays, or worked: or they can be public, for example of big events such as a coronation, or wartime images. In addition to photographs, press cuttings and scrap-books can be used. A photograph is more likely to survive the many moves a person makes in their life than other memory triggers. They can be very helpful when trying to put together key events in a life story. Requesting photographs can often be a good way of involving relatives who otherwise may feel they do not have a part to play.

Mark and Nellie look at her old family photos together and he picks out points of interest. (Bradford)

The local library is often a good source of photographs of the area as it used to be. Photos of films and film stars are also useful triggers and many older people have kept scrapbooks and cuttings about their favourite stars which can be a pleasurable source of reminiscences.

Smells

Using fresh flowers, moth balls and strong smelling cures like eucalyptus can evoke powerful emotions. The smell of a perfume or flower, roses for instance, can be introduced as a background to a reminiscence session, and need not be referred to or identified specifically. Some smells are available commercially in bottled sets, but these are difficult to use because they do not have the associated feel and look. A sprig of real lavender, a tin of *'Mansion'* polish or a bottle of 4711 perfume is more likely to bring back memories.

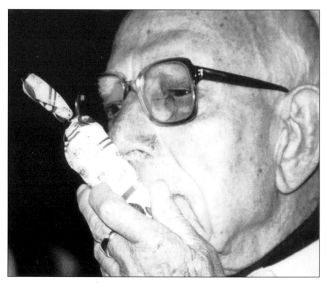

Mr. Zurburg enjoys the smell of lavender and the memories associated with it. (Amsterdam)

Textures

Some textures are particularly reminiscent of certain periods in people's lives. For some people, especially those who find it difficult to communicate verbally, the feel of a fur coat, satin dress, or velvet may be pleasurable to touch and evocative of their younger 'going out' days. The feel of different textures such as silver, sand, sacking or wood can be enjoyed for themselves, but with the sensation may also come associated memories, actions and perhaps long-forgotten words connected with working days, or places lived in or objects owned.

> **"***Marie had been a star dancer in her younger days. When her children were born she stopped dancing for ever and devoted herself entirely to her family. This was obviously a cause of some regret throughout her life and her son told me that she had made him feel guilty about it. During one session, the group brought along photographs of themselves and their families and looked at them together. Marie had no photos and said very little. At the end of the session, I put a large photo of a Degas painting of a dancer into her hand and asked if she would like to keep it. She smiled and thanked me. This picture is now beside her bed and is the only picture in her otherwise bare room.* **"**

Group leader, Paris

May and Edith are exploring a box full of fabrics and shiny objects connected with dressing up and looking good. Joyce, a volunteer, is supporting them (London)

Taste

The taste of particular food and drinks can be strongly associated with memories, especially if they are tastes not recently experienced. Old types of sweets, licorice sticks or aniseed balls, or recipes from the 1920's or 1930's such as junket, tripe and onions or bread with dripping, can remind people of their childhood and early years.

Sounds

Sounds can be used to take people back to a place or a time in their lives and can be very successful in evoking feelings and memories. Local libraries may have tapes of sounds, for example, of bird song, wild geese, the sea, wind, horses hooves, church bells or trains.

The rhythms and rhymes of old proverbs or well-worn phrases will easily come to mind in a group where many people are there to help find the missing words.These phrases are often a useful trigger for remembering the important people in one's past life and when they used to use these phrases.

Music

Music acts as a very powerful trigger for many people. Again the more information leaders can have about an individual's interest and taste the more successful they are likely to be in triggering memories using music.

> **"A participant was singing a song which moved another member to tears. The singer stopped and apologised, but the tearful member begged her to carry on as the emotion was powerful in a positive way and she was not afraid of it."**
>
> **London**

Tom loves the music of the Dubliners and here he is joining in by marking the rhythm and singing some lines of one of his favourite numbers played by a visiting musician. (Bradford)

Listening to music can evoke memories of places, times, occasions and people. This is particularly so if the music is played live or on authentic equipment. It can also bring back the feelings and strong emotions associated with the memories. These feelings may not always be happy ones, but if the group is supportive, expressing the sorrow can be therapeutic.

"Jim was a quiet shy man from Glasgow who did not find it easy to contribute his memories to the group. One week he mentioned that he had always enjoyed big band music. The leader was able to go to the library and borrow several CD's of big band music, including some by well-known Scottish band leaders. The following week they played extracts from some of these, bringing back many memories for Jim and others in the group. Finding and playing music that he enjoyed made Jim feel that people were interested in him as an individual and listening to it with other members helped him to feel more fully a part of the group".

Bradford

Group leaders can use music to change the mood of a meeting or to engage members in activities involving movement and dance. Photocopies of songs in large print can be helpful for some people. Singing together is often a good way to bring people together and develop a sense of comradeship. Some people who find speech difficult may remember the words of songs learned long ago, especially if others are there to help. They may only remember fragments or occasional phrases, but this will enable them to sing along and feel that they are contributing to the group experience.

Movement

Sometimes actions can trigger memories. Giving people the opportunity to make actions or movements associated with familiar rituals or work can be a good way of bringing back memories. When handling a typewriter, using a rubbing board or dancing to a piece of music, the body may recognise a familiar action and remember it even though the words may be lacking. This can be a manageable way for the person with dementia to show that they are following the main thrust of the group activity and enjoying it, even though they may not be able to verbalise this. Gestures and movements associated with religious rituals and prayer may also evoke many memories and past competencies.

Even those who can no longer recall the words of songs enjoy whistling or tapping out the rhythm of the music. (London)

The Creative Exploration of Memories

This section looks at ways of actively engaging people in creative activities related to the memories they are sharing. The emphasis is on group exercises which enable people to connect with one another's experiences and which often lead to a shareable event or outcome. Memories can be explored in a number of different ways which celebrate a person's unique life experience and give it added value. Working with a memory, turning it into a scene, a picture, a display, can stimulate the person to tell us more, perhaps spontaneously recalling long-forgotten details in response to listeners' interest and encouragement. Bringing it to life in a new form gives it a new focus and importance.

Enacting, writing about, or drawing a memory often makes it part of a new and rather special shared event in the present. It then becomes a memory belonging to the group as well as to the individual. If the event is recorded on video or in photos, this can make it easier to hold on to and enjoy again later. If there is a tangible product, such as a drawing, a painting or poem, this can be taken home and referred back to after the event to re-stimulate the original memory and the creative use that was made of it. Skillful acting or painting are not required. It is the doing of it which makes it worthwhile and memorable, not the product.

Drawing memories following a lively discussion in our comfortable reminiscence flat. (Brussels.)

We made a collage of photos of all the people in our group when we were young and we also kept a photographic record of our meetings to remind members of our joint history. (Brussels)

Photography

Members are likely to have old photographs to show to the rest of the group and these can be a good source of reminiscences. However photos taken in the first half of the 20th century may be very small and difficult for some older people to see. By enlarging images, all the detail in people's faces, clothing and settings emerges again. These enlargements can be done photographically or on a high quality laser photocopier or scanned through a computer. They can be used in a number of ways to elicit memories.

Making a group display of photos around a theme is a good way to generate strong group feeling. If the group leader announces a subject well in advance so that participants have time to look out suitable photos or contact relatives who may have them, a good display can be mounted reflecting the variety of experience within the group. If original photographs are used they need to be protected under glass or perspex. Such a display could include related items such as advertising materials, bills, postcards, etc.

Photographs can form the basis for a collage and can be added to as the group continues. Photographs of participants when they were young, and of other significant people or events in their lives, can be collected and photocopied. The resulting images can then be manipulated by group members, who may cut and paste and add colour and other items to create a joint collage. This could include fabrics and small objects. These collages may also be made by individuals working with one or two others.

A collage is made around the life of an individual, working closely with that person over a period of time. The resulting visual image prompts positive feelings and can be shared with others, offering a stimulus for further conversation. This collage was made by Karen Jarvis, Community Psychiatric Nurse in Hull, UK

A photographic record of the events and activities of the group from week to week offers members a useful means of reminding them of the enjoyable times they have passed together. Photographs can be referred back to, acting as prompts to revisit and re-enjoy the original memories and the activities stimulated by them. In Brussels, they added each week to their photo gallery and it became a useful way to remember the activities they had shared in previous meetings. It was a way of creating a shared history and a sense of continuity for the group.

Slide shows are an ideal way of sharing photos in a group. If it is possible to darken the room, one can create a special atmosphere in which members lose self-consciousness and feel very relaxed and comfortable about commenting spontaneously on each photo. Everyone can look at the same image and the detail is clear and large enough to be enjoyed by all participants.

> **"The greatest success during joint meetings were slides of old black and white photographs. Projected very large in a darkened room, they concentrated everyone's attention producing some very lively reminiscence."**
>
> **Helsinki**

Sound and Music

Recorded sound effects can be a powerful evocation of a remembered scene, but these 'real' sounds may not correspond to people's memories and are not always easily recognised. They are more likely to work if the scene has also been set in other ways, for example with images or objects.

Another approach is to ask group members to make their own sounds to represent such things as the sea, the cry of a gull, cats and dogs, a merry-go-round, trains, street-cries, etc.

Making a sound collage using different objects and vocal effects can be fun and a good way to start a session. It is also a useful way for people to contribute for whom speech is difficult. The leader sets the scene and asks members of the group to talk about the associated sounds and to think about how to reproduce them. The group can then be 'conducted' by the group leader who gives everyone a turn and combines the different sounds inviting people to become louder or softer in turn.

Recorded popular vocal or instrumental music can be used to encourage the group to bring back memories of where they were when a particular song or piece of music was played. It can re-create a place, for example a dance hall, and may bring back associated memories. Some participants may get up and enjoy dancing. Members who cannot dance themselves can listen to the music, watch the action and feel part of what is happening. From time to time, the group leader can stop the music for a short time and ask people what or who they are remembering.

A member of our group who is over 90 enjoyed playing the piano during our sessions. His repertoire expanded during the project. For example, when I sang "Night and Day" with him, he found he could play it. (Finland)

"During one meeting, my father spoke about his childhood, his school time and his working life. Suddenly he saw the piano standing there and he started playing it. I was astonished how many melodies he could still play, When I was a child, he played very often for relaxation after work."

Carer, Vienna

Live singing and recitation of old rhymes from childhood can be enjoyable for the group. Songs from early childhood can spark shared memories or memories of difference, depending on where one grew up. It is a short move from singing skipping songs, counting games and circle games to showing the actions which accompany them. Playing out old rituals of childhood choosing games, for example in the U.K., *'One potato, two potato, three potato four'*, played with fists in a circle to choose who stays in a game and who is out creates a lot of energy and good humour.

Drawing, Painting and Modelling

Many people feel they are no good at drawing or painting and are reluctant to have a go. However, if a relaxed atmosphere can be created in which the memories evoked are more important than the artistic merit of what is produced, then the process of painting and drawing can be fun. It should be stressed that "pin men" and diagrammatic representations are absolutely acceptable. If there is initial resistance, another helper can listen to a person's experience and try to draw it for them, changing the image as more information is added, almost like a visual conversation and a good way of sparking fresh memories as the detail is added into the picture.

A carer draws a recently retrieved memory while others ask questions to prompt further detailed recollection. (Brussels)

Some people in the group will be happy to do their own drawing, and then the role of the helper is to ask questions and show interest in what is being produced. The whole point of this activity is that it should be without pressure or deadline so that the process is enjoyed to the full. Any questions should be sensitively put so that concentration is not lost.

"We started talking about the grandparents' house and garden. While I was drawing, Mother filled in more and more details, for instance, where she slept, where Granny used to sit on an ordinary chair in the garden next to a rose bush, where they used to have coffee and where the apple tree was. She was very pleased and excited."

Stockholm

A drawing by Edith, aged 90, of the street in the mining village she remembers from childhood. (London)

Painting can be used as a freeing medium. It can be enjoyed as an expression of memory in a very general sense, for instance, when talking about the seaside, the colours associated with the topic can be freely applied either by participants or on their behalf by volunteers, creating colourful images for the whole group to enjoy.

The drawing or painting of an object of special significance, for example a favourite toy or well used work tool, will take some time and during that time feelings about that object can be shared in a safe way with another. For some people, drawing is a means of explaining a point when words do not readily come. If the venue allows the freedom to make a bit of a mess

and water is available, the use of clay can be very enjoyable for members of any group. Objects or figures can be modelled or the clay itself and the handling of it enjoyed. It can be rolled out and used in various imaginary ways, for example as if cooking, or to make a remembered piece of jewellery, or flattened and used to pierce or press a pattern or design onto.

> **In the third session we used clay. As soon as the clay was brought out they immediately took to it. Lily made a beautiful old woman, Louise made some shapes. All joined in reminiscing and the focus of making allowed them to talk even more freely.**
>
> **Alec told more about growing up in Poland. He has had a painful life which he had kept hidden previously, but during the course of the sessions he has shared fragments with us which were particularly moving because of this.**

An Age Exchange reminiscence project with people with dementia in a Jewish residential home for people with dementia, London

> **Leslie had organised a cinematographic club in the past. He was trying to tell a volunteer how the sprocket holes on a piece of film were threaded on to the projector. He found this very difficult. When he was offered a pen and paper, he was able to describe the mechanism successfully through a drawing, which gave him great satisfaction.**

London

Drama

Making short scenes from people's stories can be an enjoyable group activity. Suggestions for additional lines of dialogue or alternative actions can be added by those watching. Different people in the group can be invited to take over the roles. Using stock roles such as strict teacher, angry mum, unreasonable boss, stroppy pupil or worker will give plenty of people the chance to chip in. Interventions can be short so that contributors do not feel they have failed if they run out of ideas. The facilitator needs to be quick to resume the initiative and maintain confidence.

Drama can feel like a somewhat threatening medium to those who are unfamiliar with it, but it has proved very successful in RYCT and other groups involving older people with dementia. It is certainly worth trying out this approach with a group and, if it is not immediately successful, trying it on another occasion or with another group. Most activities are more successful as the leader become more confident. What seems unpromising in one group may turn out to be very successful in another.

"I found that several members of my group were resistant to drama and role play, which made enactments an uphill struggle. We used other approaches to creative exploration, but I was aware that some individuals in the group really enjoyed this activity and could have done more. I now feel more confident and would pursue the drama approach more determinedly with a second group."

Group leader
Bradford

Using drama to recreate a memory or experience can involve very small interventions, perhaps even a single word, from each participant to evoke a place or an event. It does not need to be a full-scale performance. For example, the group leader might introduce the idea of making a classroom come alive in their session and ask the group what would need to be there to make it feel like a classroom of their childhood. Then everyone would be asked to pitch in with one word suggestions, such as a blackboard, chalk, a cane, a map of the world showing the Empire, an abacus, a daffodil plant, dip-in pens, etc. Then the teacher could be put in the scene, described, again with one word suggestions as to clothes and attitude. Then she could be given things to say to the class, suggested by members of the group. It

is a short hop from this to a small scene involving the group leader as teacher or naughty child and another member of the group willing to play out a short scene based on a memory. This kind of participatory scene making raises the emotional temperature of the group and increases the air of fun and excitement.

The drama can be more of a guided fantasy where the leader conjures up an imaginary scenario for the group to fill out with their own contributions. In this example, nobody needs to get up, and the whole group work together on the exercise.

"The group leader began the session with a tape of seaside sounds while they all relaxed and listened.

She then began to set the scene by inviting everyone to imagine they were going to the seaside: "Let us suppose that we are going on an outing to the seaside in the days when we were young, I wonder where we might choose to go and what we might take with us. How will we travel? Is it a sunny or a rainy day? What might we do when we get there? What sounds might we hear? What sights will we see? What will we eat and drink? When will we leave? What might we sing on the way home?"

The questions were then asked a second time, and in the gaps between each question, everybody contributed their ideas and suggestions, as much or as little as they wished."

London

Another approach would be where group members work in small groups and explore their memories connected to a topic of shared interest. Members of the small groups listen to each other's stories and decide if one is particularly suitable for making into a scene, or if they might combine the stories into a shared memory enactment.

Participants then work together to develop a small scene in which they can all have a part and which can then be shown to the rest of the group. Performing such enactments, however basic they may be, energises the whole group and can be very amusing and enjoyable. It also has a powerful effect on those watching and often spontaneously evokes long-forgotten memories of similar situations.

Acting out seaside memories. (London)

Not all drama needs words. Miming an action (perhaps with a commentary) can be just as effective and can lead to all sorts of guessing games about what is going on. The audience will read different things into these actions and will enjoy watching and responding. An example of this approach might be miming the first job you had.

Props and costumes can help with dramatising. For example, having a deck chair, a towel or a bucket and spade might help a seaside enactment or hats of various kinds might help with a market or street scene. Handling the props and costumes can be fun for group members who may not be able to take a very active part in the enactment.

> 66*Harry, a carer, tells the group that when he was about seven he 'borrowed' his grandad's false teeth and brought them to school for a laugh. The teacher found out and his mother was sent for. He had to go home in disgrace. Gael, another carer, plays the teacher, Harry plays himself and the volunteer plays his mother. They practise and then act the scene for the whole group.*99

Bradford

Practising old skills

It can be a positive experience to revisit familiar actions from the past. It may sound strange to say that the body has a memory, but some people with dementia enjoy trying again and remembering physical actions connected to past abilities. Although they may no longer be able to type forty letters a day, handling an old typewriter and feeling the keys under their fingers is a powerful reminder of past competence.

Again, baking for the entire family may no longer be an option, but feeling the wooden spoon beating against the side of the bowl is a pleasurable reminder of all the cakes successfully baked in the past. It is also a means of evoking memories of being a wife and mother. Where a reminiscence group prepares food, using traditional recipes, and then enjoys eating it together, a great sense of fellowship and party spirit can be engendered.

> 66*The group handled household objects they had used competently in their adult life, and as they did so, they remembered the actions associated with those objects. One member held a heavy flat iron and remembered how she had taken it from the fire. She pretended it was very hot as she picked it up and she pressed it down as though she was actually ironing. This was a pleasurable memory. Another group member was handling the peat blocks which were used to keep a fire alight overnight. His wife was able to describe the way they were used. He had fewer words, but he showed by the way he handled the blocks that he remembered too.*99

Amsterdam

Handling items of equipment, for instance sewing machines or old tools, can also be a means for members of the group to experience again important roles they have played in their lives and these can then be shared with the group.

However, it is important to know members well before introducing such tasks, especially where there is an element of potential failure. For individuals who can no longer carry out the actions, being confronted with something they cannot do will be unhelpful. We do not want to remind people with dementia of the gap between what they used to be able to do and what they can do now.

Re-using old skills and handling the sewing machine again can be pleasurable and confidence-building. (Oslo)

Life story work

This can take many forms from a simple file with photographs and information to a more elaborate and creative piece of work. It can be in the form of a booklet with photos, captions and cuttings, or a collage using photographs, writing, and drawing, or it can be 3-dimensional as in a Memory Box. It can reflect a lifetime or just a particular corner of someone's life which they want to remember.

How complicated and ambitious a project it is, will depend on the time available, how much the person with dementia is able to contribute in terms of their own memories about the past, and whether the person making the life story can contact and get information and help from family and friends. It can be

> **"One of the participants was very anxious at the beginning of the project. Then we did some practical household chores in our meetings, baking, washing and sewing. After the second such meeting, she said, "Next time I'd better bring my apron with me and do the job here. Funny really, I thought it was you who should do this for me. I have done this all my life, but I had better show you, you youngsters ..." And she pointed at the group leaders."**

Oslo

made over a number of days or weeks, or over a longer period with new memories and stories being added as they emerge. It may be made in a day centre where the person with dementia attends or at home by the carer. In the latter case, it may work better if another person, a neighbour or friend, can help. Their extra encouragement may help the person with dementia to tell their stories to a new *'audience'* and become more actively involved in the process.

Memory boxes

Making a Memory Box is another way of recording and displaying a person's memories. It is a process which takes quite a long time and requires some practical skills. An appropriate box or other suitable container first needs to be found or made. It needs to be strong enough to hold whatever is selected and have sides to which photos or small objects can be attached.

Life story books are made for and with individual clients. (Amsterdam)

The maker needs to work with the person with dementia over several sessions in order to find the best way of visually representing their memories and experiences. If the making of the box can be a joint effort, actively involving the person with dementia in selecting, making and painting items for inclusion, it will be much more satisfying for both parties. It may be an opportunity to make contact with family or friends of the person with dementia to ask for suitable items to help jog memories and to fill out the boxes with relevant materials reflecting the life story. If several people make a box, the resulting display is fascinating as it highlights the individuality of the 'makers' and generates interest and mutual engagement.

Memory Boxes: one person has made a theatre out of her box and sees her life as a series of scenes and stages; the other person dedicates her box to her parents and shows how they took in extra sewing and cobbling work and cared for her as a child through years of poverty. (London)

"*A young artist who worked on a series of such Memory Boxes in London found the activity fascinating. It stretched her imagination considerably to find the right arrangement of photos and objects and to make missing items or scenery which would bind together the disparate elements in the box into a coherent whole.*
*"I really started to understand how important memories are. Helping people to remember a lot of things that they have done in the past, recalling forgotten times - happy or sad - seems to remind them of who they are and give them a renewed sense of identity. People are so special and everyone deserves the time to be listened to and appreciated."***"**

Age Exchange, London

Bringing Reminiscence into Daily Life At Home

Reminiscence can be a valuable tool for stimulating communication on a daily basis. This section aims to give family carers, volunteers and others ideas about a range of practical activities to try in or around the home environment which are enjoyable for all concerned.

We recognise that the onset of dementia can lead those involved to reduce their social contacts with others. Reluctance to invite people into the home or to take a person with dementia into a public place because of fear of embarrassment is entirely understandable, but it can lead to serious lack of stimulation for both the person with dementia and their carer. Often friends or relatives who would like to help are unsure about what to do, or what contribution to make. Reminiscence can be both a way of giving a new focus to long-standing relationships, and a basis on which new ones can be formed. Some of the activities in this section can be tried at home, and others involve outings to places linked with the past.

See reminiscence as a potential tonic - a little every day can help generate a feeling of well-being.

❝A volunteer asks Pedro, "Do you remember this copper kettle?". Pedro looks at the kettle, which is in the middle of one of the shelves of the dining-room sideboard.

He picks it up, touches it, looks me in the eyes, smiles and stammeringly replies "Fantoxin - market, Barbastro. Micaela" I look at Micaela (Pedro's wife) and she looks at me wonderingly, very surprised, and says "About fifteen years ago, one summer we were near Barbastro. One Saturday we went to the market and bought this kettle. We've almost never mentioned it. How can he remember it?" Pedro said with a smile "She liked it a lot"❞

Barcelona

Using objects around the home

A useful starting point for carers is to look round the person with dementia's home and recognise potential reminiscence triggers, for example, old photos on walls or in albums, holiday souvenirs, ornaments and gifts, trophies and certificates, old wedding or birthday gifts. All these can be a source for reminiscence for the family carer and others who visit the home such as home helps, paid carers who spend time in the house, or visiting friends and relatives.

❝A daughter arranged a reminiscence journey through her mother's apartment with objects and memorabilia. It consisted of 'elements of favoured activities such as kitchen work, knitting, reading the bible, hugging a puppet, and examining memorabilia connected to her previous nurse training'.❞

Kirkheim/Teck

Taking out an old stamp album or other hobby book can stimulate memories of the activity, the times when the activity was pursued, and remembered knowledge associated with the activity. (Helsinki)

Looking at old photographs together can be pleasurable for people with dementia and their carers. If photographs are labelled and the labels are read out this can reduce any anxiety on the part of the person with dementia about not recognising the people or places in the photos.

> **"A carer told us,"Yesterday I looked with mother at old photographs of hers when she was eighteen or nineteen years old. I wanted to learn about what they showed and she was still able to tell me about them, to explain! It was a lovely feeling for mother and for me as well."**
>
> **Leuven**

Carers might select a few objects or photos and put them out on a table when visitors are expected.

Some of these could be objects which remind the person with dementia of their past, but may also be played with by visiting grandchildren, for example, a toy or game.

The carer could select different objects and photographs to put in the person with dementia's handbag or briefcase every day, and time could be set aside to explore and enjoy the contents together.

It isn't always easy to spot the potential of photos or objects which have been around for many years. So any visitor to the home may bring a fresh pair of eyes if they are invited to help stimulate reminiscence. They may even bring objects themselves.

Another contribution which visiting relatives can make is to talk through shared memories, with the person with dementia and the carer adding their memories. Old letters and postcards may also be brought out and shared again, as can presents brought back from past holidays with all their associated memories.

Helping to maintain contact with family and friends

Often relatives or friends who have lost touch or who are uncertain how to maintain the relationship in the new more difficult situation, are happy to give help in the form of written or spoken memories. They may then gain the confidence to re-establish regular contact with the carer and the person with dementia.

With preparation, a telephone call can provide stimulating conversations and help maintain contact with friends and relatives.

> **"Since Tom became ill, contact with his two grown-up children from a first marriage had been increasingly difficult to maintain. Although Tom obviously missed seeing and hearing from them, his wife, Gael, felt reticent about contacting them and unsure whether they wanted to keep in touch. Involvement in a reminiscence project gave her a practical reason for writing to ask for recollections to help stimulate Tom. An eight page letter received in response two days later showed how much they cared about their dad and how pleased they were to be able to help. The family is now communicating regularly again as a result."**
>
> **Bradford**

> **"One carer found a way to help her husband keep up his old friendships with people who kept in touch by phone. When an old friend rang she would ask him to ring back in ten minutes. While she was waiting for his call back she would talk to her husband about the friend. For each of his friends she found an image or a story to jog his memory, for example, 'Paul was the man who used to bring us smoked fish' … 'Karl helped us to tow the car home when it broke down that night'. In this way her husband was able to keep speaking to his friends on the phone. Otherwise he would just say, 'I don't know who this is, you had better speak to him.'"**
>
> **Kassel**

Television and films

Look at forthcoming TV and radio programmes likely to have associations, choosing together programmes which might stimulate joint memories. By remembering aloud both before and during the programme, the carer can stimulate shared memories and help the person with dementia to 'stay tuned' and enjoy the programme. The carer might make comments while watching a film, for example, *'You had a dress like that - it was one of my favourites'*, or *'Do you remember* we saw that film at the Elite?' A programme may be recorded on video, and then watched all the way through or in shorter sections with the person with dementia. The programme can be paused to leave time for comments and reactions and then may be replayed from time to time, as long as it remains a source of enjoyment.

Marking up forthcoming TV programmes which might be stimulating to watch together

❝*I used to look through the Radio and TV Times to see what programmes were coming up which would interest Ken. He was a great railway enthusiast, so whenever there were programmes featuring old trains (whether in films or documentaries) we would watch them together. I'd remind him of train journeys we'd gone on together when we went on holiday and he always brightened up after these sessions.*❞

A carer, London

Reading aloud

People with dementia often have great difficulty maintaining concentration long enough to absorb material if they are looking at it alone. However if the family carer or another sits with the person and points out pictures, news items or ideas of interest, for example in a local paper, he or she can once again enjoy keeping up with local news, and feel part of the community by doing this.

❝*We read the newspaper with our day centre members, as a means of triggering discussion about their own lives. For example, we were looking at something about bananas and people began talking about the first banana boats to arrive in Sweden in their younger days. We also read some items about the war in former Yugoslavia and this triggered a discussion about their own wartime memories.*❞

Stockholm

A carer reads aloud from a favourite book. (Brussels)

Creating familiar corners

Some people with dementia miss familiar activities which they used to do regularly in the past, for example those connected with their working life. They can find comfort in doing them again at home.

Remembering working days as a shoe-maker by handling the original tools (Amsterdam)

Making a memory box, life story or scrap book

A life story or scrap-book may also be made at home. This can be a means of reaffirming past experience, and can be enjoyed by both the carer and the person with dementia. It could contain photographs and stories, or be in the form of a scrap-book with photographs, cuttings and captions recording important events and people in the life of the person with dementia.

> **She looks into the reminiscence book I have made for her and remembers people and talks about them. I have no problems talking with her, because I know her world. The project has helped me come closer into her life. The reminiscence book is on her writing bureau. She likes it.**
>
> **Carer, Copenhagen**

A 3-dimensional Memory Box is another way of collecting and displaying a person's life. The carer and the person with dementia can gradually collect together items such as photos, small objects, materials in different colours, souvenirs, medals and trophies, and arrange them in an interesting way. (see page 33 for more details).

The enjoyment of the process of making a Memory Box or life story book is as important as the end product. It should not be rushed!

Kit, aged 80, made this memory box out of an old supermarket box. As a girl, she loved to go hop picking in the Kent countryside. The family slept in cattlesheds which they lined with wallpaper and made quite cosy. Kit had assembled small replica objects, including a tiny woollen blanket which she knitted herself to re-evoke these happy memories. (London)

A pictorial or written record can help others who may later spend time with the person with dementia to get to know them when they may no longer be able to remember or recount details about their past life themselves.

Re-enjoying photo albums

New captions could be added to an old photo album, or photos rearranged, perhaps making a book for grandchildren or younger relatives. Perhaps the carer or younger members of the family have access to a computer and could type captions adding to them as new memories arise. A loose-leaf pocket file could be used to make the process flexible. Some families have slides or cine-films which could be enjoyed again with grandchildren, neighbours or friends. As well as bringing back memories, looking at old photographs and films might trigger discussions about how daily life has changed.

The pleasure of leafing through an old photo album. (Brussels)

Bringing old routines into current life

Sometimes old routines may be more acceptable than current ones. For example, someone who had a bath on Fridays at some point in life may find baths more acceptable if reminded of his old routine.

Old jokes and catch phrases may be a way in to old feelings of familiarity and security. Remembering these and using them at points in the current routine can give moments of real contact between carer and person.

> **L. smiles in recognition when I use words and expressions which we used in fun years ago.**
>
> **Helsinki**

Going out on visits

The carer and person with dementia can spend some time visiting favourite haunts enjoyed in the past such as school buildings, cinemas visited jointly in courting days, a favourite pub or cafe, a place of work or worship. All these can stimulate memories and constitute a pleasurable joint activity.

This activity can apply equally to the carer or the person with dementia as well as memories shared by both. A person with dementia may be used to being the listener or accompanying the carer on their outings, and may prefer this role.

> **Harry (carer) took his wife Winifred on a trip back to the village where he had been born. They spent the day exploring, with Harry saying things like 'round the corner there used to be a such and such' and then he and Winifred looking to see if it was still there. Reminiscence provided a purpose and framework to the day, and although they were Harry's memories, Winifred was able to share all Harry's pleasure in them.**
>
> **Bradford**

A visit to a museum - especially where the exhibits reflect the life experience of ordinary people of this century, can provide a rich source of stimulation and memories. Many museums have collections drawn from the local area, which provide especially relevant triggers for many participants.

> **The Industrial Museum has two back-to-back houses, one furnished with items from the early 1900's, and the other from the 1930's to 1940's. The group visited the museum and sat in the kitchen of one of the houses.**
>
> **A member of staff from the museum passed objects round for everyone to enjoy. The furniture, chairs, sink, old range, and decoration took everyone back to when they were young. In another part of the museum the group saw working mill machinery and stables with shire horses, which many people remembered.**
>
> **Bradford**

Car boot sales and second hand shops

These are good places to browse and look for objects which can be bought cheaply either because they bring back memories or just because they catch the eye. It is also enjoyable just to handle old objects free from the usual constraints of a shop. People are often more friendly and are willing to talk about the past life of an object (if they happen to know it) with the person with dementia. This kind of informal conversation, which is often missing, is very 'normalising' and can make the person with dementia feel more integrated into everyday life and more accepted.

A carer and his wife pay a visit to an exhibition of household objects at a local museum. (Amsterdam)

Funfairs, livestock markets, markets, seaside and countryside visits

Arriving in a different place with different sounds and a fresh view can lift the spirits. Enjoy the food and drink associated with these visits, for example, a pub lunch, a river boat trip with beer, fish and chips, shell fish, candy floss and cream teas.

Take a grandchild along and enjoy joint activities, such as making sand pies or sand castles, paddling, bird watching, picking wild flowers, collecting pebbles on the beach.

Pick wild flowers and press them between sheets of blotting paper in a book. These could later be made into an album.

Look for shells on the beach, collect them, and take them home to enjoy later. The feel and the colour of the shells and the sounds of the sea in some of them can bring back memories of the outing.

Go for local walks, and use the walks to establish a

"My husband has not got much language left, but we make the same walk every day, singing old songs and hymns. My husband touches the trees and says hello to everyone we meet."

Carer, Oslo.

familiar and enjoyable routine for the person with dementia.

Members of a project, as they get to know one another, may wish to organise trips together either as a whole group or perhaps with two carers and those they care for.

Family celebrations

Think about birthdays and other anniversaries, and try and organise an event which evokes memories. Invite family and friends to be involved in planning celebrations, which could be at home, or could involve a visit to a local special event such as a tea-dance.

One of our carers organised enjoyable outings for the whole group to places associated with happy memories. (Kassel)

Using Reminiscence in Care Settings

There are a number of good reasons for using reminiscence materials and activities in day-centres, residential and nursing homes and hospitals, or any other setting where people with dementia attend or stay.

Firstly, the use of materials from the past can help to enrich the environment. Objects and images can be displayed on walls, in entrance halls, and in lounge areas for people with dementia to enjoy. Using reminiscence in this way creates an environment which is stimulating and which can often provide a starting point for conversation or activities.

Relatives and former carers can be invited to contribute to, or be involved in, gathering materials when planning displays or reminiscence work. Even where relatives live further away, information and perhaps photographs can be sent. It can be helpful for both staff and relatives if they are able to work together in a positive and creative way on behalf of their people with dementia.

> **Now we have a mixed group of family carers and people with dementia, I talk to the carers every week. That helps me to see the 'big picture'. I see the people with dementia at the day centre every day, but now I also hear the carer's story. And I see the partners together. And the carers see how we deal with their partners and gain new ideas.**
>
> **Group leader, Amsterdam**

Reminiscence work either in small groups or one-to-one can help staff show the people with dementia that they are interested in them as individuals. The process of reminiscing then helps the staff to know their clients better and to treat them with greater understanding and respect. Spontaneous moments of reminiscence triggered perhaps by an item on display or a photograph brought in can also be very satisfying for both staff and people with dementia. More structured groupwork can be organised, with time set aside on a regular basis. This can be for a specific group of clients over a fixed period of time, or for a looser group of members with a regular meeting time, but open to anyone attending at the time the activities take place. If extra helpers can be involved, people with dementia will gain the maximum benefit from participation in a group.

Individual work using reminiscence can be especially useful with people who find communication or involvement in groups difficult. They may be withdrawn for a number of reasons. They may be depressed or shy, or have physical difficulties such as deafness or visual impairment. If staff can set aside a little time on a regular basis and find appropriate reminiscence materials to explore, this can help the person with dementia to feel valued and part of the community. It is important to find materials which will trigger the person's interest, and which will stimulate as many senses as possible, including touch, smell, taste, sound and sight.

Reminiscence provides a starting point and a structure. It creates a focus for a range of activities which use the past as a way of enjoying communication in the present. It helps individuals, both those with dementia and staff, to connect with each other and make satisfying social relationships. Exploring the past can provide firm ground on which new social relationships can be made, helping people with dementia to get to know and enjoy the company of others. It is likely that this will require some help from staff who may be in a position to make the initial links between people, on the basis of what they have learned about them through informal reminiscence conversations. Such links can form the start of a continuing friendship or sense of association. Using objects, music and photographs can also be a good way of helping people to relax and get to know each other.

Gathering photographs

These can be early photographs from individuals and photographs from the present, from trips or from enjoyable sessions. Photographs of familiar objects and places may also be used, mounted individually with labels underneath to make a small exhibition. For instance you could have a portrait gallery of every resident or day-centre client, using where possible one early photograph and one more recent one, both clearly labelled. Staff could also provide an early and a recent photograph for the 'exhibition'.

Collage

After reminiscence sessions where individuals talk about themselves when they were younger, any photographs gathered or borrowed could be photocopied and then a group collage could be made. This might be made using only photographic images or using a combination of photographs and fabrics, drawings, stories and objects. If a person has no photograph from when they were younger, or no relatives or friends who could help obtain one, a recent photograph can be used.

> ”Merry-go-rounds; funfair; music.
> Fishy kippers smell fatty
> Seaweed; salty swishy waves.
> Stormy ... thunder, lightning, windy.
> Eels, ships, people's voices.
> Vinegar; cars going up and down fast.
> Fine shovelling sand, and oily sweet

A table of memories

A selection of objects and images can be laid out for clients and staff to enjoy. The display can be changed on a regular basis and may be a general collection or a group of objects on a specific theme. An example might be a table with an old silk shawl, powder compact, gentleman's shaving set, gloves, 4711 toilet water, copies of photographs of a local dance hall, theatre or cafe, a pair of silk stockings and an evening bag.

Objects may be found in local second hand shops, borrowed from local museums or libraries, or loaned or given by relatives or friends of staff and clients. If they are delicate or precious they may need to be displayed under glass.

A trail of objects

Objects could be placed in a trail between different areas where people with dementia move. These could be home or work-related and could reflect the interests of those people with dementia currently attending the

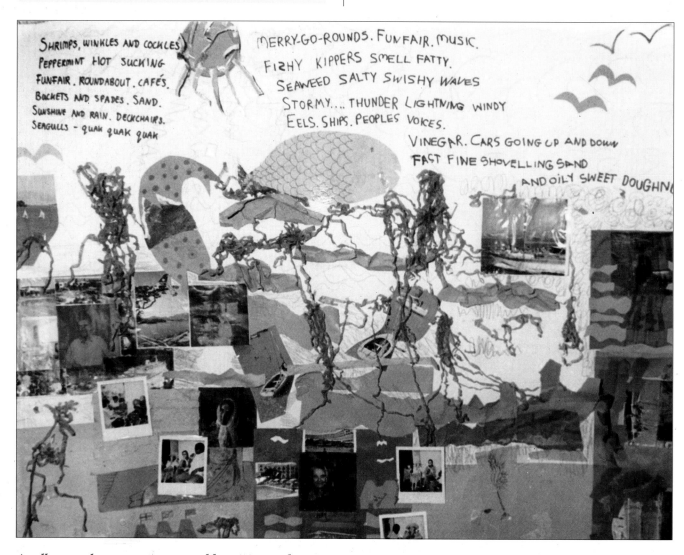

A collage and group poem created by an Age Exchange reminiscence group with people with dementia at Hackney Hospital (London)

day-centre or living in the home. If these objects have been used in reminiscence sessions and comments made by those handling them have been recorded, the comments could be written on cards as quotes with the name of the person who was talking, and placed by the object. For example a typewriter might have been enjoyed by someone who used to be a secretary and their comments could be placed in paper on the keyboard: 'I was one of the fastest. I used to type for Mr Smith and he was very particular. In those days if you made a mistake, you had to do it all over again'. Involving people with dementia in collecting, labelling or placing the objects will be enjoyable in itself. The objects will be enjoyed by clients and staff, and by anyone visiting, and can provide a topic of conversation.

Using reminiscence in daily routines

Objects and phrases can be used to liven up daily routines, and to reduce potential moments of tension. Singing songs from the past at bath-time for instance can be fun for both carer and the person with dementia.

Finding out from spouses or previous carers what the person with dementia used to enjoy doing can help to ensure that as far as possible familiar and preferred routines are followed. Sometimes this might involve remembering what happened in the person with dementia's very early life, for example Mum saying 'night night, sleep tight', or 'sweet dreams' or all kneeling for a goodnight prayer with parents or brothers and sisters.

Toys and other objects from childhood can be a source of comfort to the person with dementia and allow them to show affection. (UK)

Using phrases or routines from a person's early childhood does not mean that you treat a person with dementia like a child; only that you recognise that some songs or words from the past may be comforting and helpful to the person with dementia in the present.

Ivy and daycare staff take a break after a painting session. (London)

An RYCT Project in a Paris Nursing Home

An evaluation of the RYCT reminiscence workshops with residents of a Jewish nursing home and their carers at Maison de Retraite et de Geriatrie, Fondation de Rothschild, Paris by Arlette Goldberg, Co-ordinator of Social Life and RYCT group leader

For the ten weekly sessions of this reminiscence workshop (following the approach taught at Age Exchange Reminiscence Centre, London) we gathered eight nursing home residents and some of their children-carers, into a rather homogenous group: all came originally from Eastern Europe and all had light to moderate symptoms of dementia.

Through the recall of their past daily life and events, emphasising the happiest and earliest memories, and with the help of various supports such as objects, photographs, songs, dance, smells and tastes) we explored a range of themes. These included the Seder (Passover) celebrations remembered from childhood, a favourite dress, school days, a beautiful landscape remembered, a wonderful journey, the first job, washing linen, courting and marriage, cakes and other favourite recipes.

The results have been recognised by the children-carers as very positive for their parent and for themselves as well. For the residents, the workshops resulted in a more positive mood and an easier communication, in a stronger sense of identity and a better integration in the home. The pleasure of meeting and sharing good memories has been stronger than the sadness in recalling tragic war memories. Children-carers have stated that the communication with their parents in the workshops facilitated the following outcomes:

1) possibility of being happy and relaxed with them, despite their dementia

Arlette Goldberg with her group of residents and family members. (Paris)

2) discovering memories they had never heard before, among which were memories of a Jewish past, hidden by one mother traumatised by the Shoah

2) the possibility of sharing experiences with other carers

4) the pleasure of coming to the sessions

5) the pleasure of seeing an improvement in the spirits of other carees

6) disappointment because the workshop does not go on through the whole year

7) intention on the part of carers to continue *"in some way"* with the group reminiscing or doing something else together

8) proposals by most of the carers to offer their services as volunteers in the nursing home, whether in connection with this group or outside it.

Reminiscence has been experienced as:

1) confirming the sense of identity and self-worth

2) encouraging sociability

3) transmitting what has not yet been transmitted

4) creating a more equal relationship through reminiscence work together

5) creating a sense of cohesion and friendship

8) in some cases, helping to overcome depression, among carers no less than among carees.

The therapeutic aspect of this workshop has been emphasised and endorsed by the chief physician-geriatrist of the home after the end of the workshop.

He states that

"The results are impressive and quite conclusive. The carers have found new ways of relating, not only to their parent, but to other carers too, and they have decided to invest a lot more personal effort.

They are less upset by their parents' ageing and they seem to put more value on their past life experience. The people with dementia have found a greater sense of self acceptance, and the moments of emotion they have had the opportunity to go through have helped them to re-socialise with fellow residents."

**Dr Serge Reingewirtz,
Fondation Rothschild, Paris**

Running a Reminiscence Project

This section includes ideas about setting up and running a reminiscence project. It highlights some of the issues which need to be considered in order to get started, such as ensuring that there is a willing project team, sufficient funds, a suitable venue, clear aims and objectives, and a potential group of participants. It goes on to consider how to maintain the momentum of the project, building in procedures for monitoring and evaluation, and planning for the group's closure.

There is no one way to run a group. Flexibility and sensitivity are more important than anything else when planning and running any reminiscence group, but especially one catering for people with dementia. Each group must address the specific needs and strengths of the individuals involved, finding out what works well for them.

Getting going

A reminiscence project takes time, needs leadership, participants, helpers and a venue. There may well be funding implications, in which case commitment from managers and support from co-workers is essential. You may need to convince others of the value of reminiscence in general, and this approach in particular. You will need to argue convincingly that your project will be beneficial for the client group and for the organisation as a whole. In making your case it may be helpful to draw on the experience of the RYCT project which found that there were benefits to staff as well as participants (see summary of conclusions to RYCT Evaluation Report on page 67). If a cost-benefits analysis is needed, it may be helpful to include involvement in a project as an element in staff training and development.

A significant feature of the RYCT project is the emphasis on having people from different disciplines working together. If you can find an enthusiastic partner from a different field - e.g. a community arts worker, a photographer, librarian, or drama specialist - with whom to collaborate, this will add a new dimension to the work. Also it makes sense to work as closely as possible with local people active in the field of dementia care, as they will help to ensure that potential participants are invited to join a group at a time when they are best able to benefit from it.

Basic practical considerations can make a big difference to willingness to participate. For some carers on a restricted budget, or those for whom public transport

Our group met in the early evening as many of the carers were still at work. In this way we combined our meetings with a light meal and this added to the sociability of the occasion. (Leuven)

is difficult, free door-to-door transport may be necessary if they are to join a group. Where projects are hoping to involve family carers in some separate carer-only sessions, provision may have to be made for those they care for to be looked after during these times. This might be through a respite care agency or, where carers are unhappy to leave their person behind, it would be even better to have enough helpers to work with the people with dementia in a nearby room while carers are meeting, so that they too feel part of the project and get used to attending regularly.

When designing a project you need to build in plans for measuring its effectiveness. This will be useful both for those involved in the project, and those who are authorising or observing it from the outside. Funders and managers are more likely to support a project which has clearly stated aims and some way of showing whether they have been met. *(See section on Monitoring and Evaluation on page 62.)*

Group planning and duration

Decisions have to be made about how often the group will meet, how many weeks it will run, and what will happen when the group finishes. It is important that this basic information is shared with all those involved in the group, and that everyone understands the extent of their commitment. Many groups find that between eight and ten sessions seems to be the right length for

"As a theatre worker with a great deal of reminiscence experience, I was nevertheless nervous about working with people with dementia and not sure which approaches would succeed. It was very reassuring to have a community psychiatric nurse and a doctor with vast experience of dementia working with me. They too gained much insight into the value of reminiscence arts as a means of communication and took their new learning back into their own fields of work"

London

the life of a reminiscence group, but this can, and often is extended if members and leaders are able and willing to continue. During this time, the major topics or themes can be addressed, although each one has the potential for considerable extension and exploration in greater depth through creative project approaches.

However, anyone setting up a project introducing reminiscence work to carers and people with dementia, will need meetings to prepare the carers and time for carers-only sessions during the project itself. Between 14 and 18 sessions altogether may be required.

One husband told us that his wife looked forward to coming to the meetings and she did not like to be left at home during these sessions for carers only, even though she had a volunteer with her for these times. (Oslo)

RYCT Project Outline

Creating the project team

including group leaders, volunteers, students and other helpers

Initial reminiscence training and preparation sessions for the team

Locating/ interviewing possible participants

18 weekly meetings lasting 2 hours

Weeks 1-4:

4 sessions for carers and volunteers

Practising reminiscence at home between sessions

(During these sessions, the people with dementia may remain at home or come along with their carers, meeting separately with volunteer support)

Weeks 5,7,9,11,13,17:

7 fortnightly 'joint' meetings for carers, volunteers/helpers and people with dementia

Weeks 6,8,10,12,14,18:

7 fortnightly review and planning meetings for carers and helpers/ volunteers

(During these sessions, the people with dementia stay at home or come along for separate sessions with volunteers/ helpers)

Work at home by family carer with their person with dementia through out the period of the project

Post-project interviews

Final evaluation of project

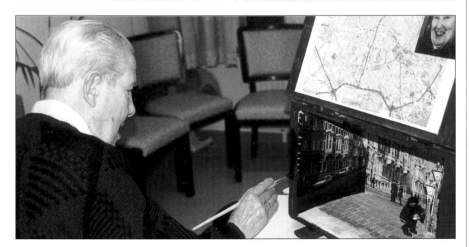

Mr. J. van Nassauw recreating his working life as a paviour in his memory box. (Amsterdam)

Group leaders and the project team

Where possible it is best to have two co-leaders, so that there can be complementary skills and mutual support. Where there is more than one leader, roles will need to be negotiated and people will need to evolve ways of working together which play to their individual strengths and personalities.

"There were three key workers on the project: an historian, an occupational therapist and a social worker. These different professions were complementary and made for a strong and flexible team learning much from one another."

It is essential to have a high ratio of helpers to participants so that individual support and stimulation is available whenever needed. Even where family carers are involved, it would be a mistake to rely exclusively on them to give this type of support. Recruit volunteers, relatives or friends to make sure this happens.

Extra helpers can be found in a number of different ways depending on local situations. Local community groups or voluntary organisations can be approached, or the group leader can advertise in a local paper.

The project could be a training placement for care staff or students. Previous experience of either dementia or reminiscence is not as important as a commitment to the aims of the project, a liking of older people, an interest in hearing stories about the past, and the ability to listen sensitively in a non-judgemental way.

It is a good idea to hold at least two preparatory meetings for leaders and helpers so that background information can be given, ideas can be shared and the aims of the group agreed. If they have not had previous experience of working with people with dementia, they may also want some information about dementia and about the communication and other difficulties carers and people with dementia face.

Preparatory meetings will help to develop a feeling of being part of a team where everyone's contribution is welcomed and valued. It is important to include some opportunities for personal reminiscence in these meetings to help the team members to get to know each other on an equal basis, and to give everyone involved a flavour of what is going to be happening in the proposed group or project.

Everyone in the project team will need time and encouragement to allow their role and potential to develop fully. Tensions between group members at the beginning of a project are natural, as individuals find their own role within the group. Part of a leader's task is to provide the confidence and flexibility for this to happen safely.

Recruitment of participants

Decisions will need to be taken about whether or not to involve family carers, and whether to limit the group to people with dementia who are at a particular point in their illness, for example, soon after diagnosis, those using services but still living in the community or those living in institutional care. Recruitment is very much affected by local circumstances, and by a project

Doris Otte interviews a carer who is interested in joining the project. (Vienna)

organiser's role and contacts. You need to find and use the most effective referral routes for your own situation. For example, it can be particularly difficult to attract recently diagnosed participants unless you have existing links with community health agencies. Some project leaders might feel that it is better to work with spouse-carers or child-carers, or to focus on people with mild dementia. However access to a larger pool of potential participants will be needed if you wish to restrict the project in this way.

Most RYCT pilot projects worked very successfully with mixed groups. Participants can enjoy differences as well as experience in common, provided the group leader is sensitive to the possible anxieties and feelings of members. Information about the very different ways in which dementia affects individuals may need to be discussed, so that members can be reassured that what they see happening to another person may not necessarily happen to them or the person they are looking after.

With individual attention and thought, even those with quite severe disabilities can benefit a great deal from being part of a group, and should not necessarily be excluded on these grounds alone. For example a volunteer or worker can sit next to a person who has hearing difficulties and help them to follow what is happening, by speaking loudly and giving visual clues. Someone who is blind may also enjoy being in a group but will need more opportunities to handle objects, and the help of someone who can describe the contents of photographs or other images. Similarly an individual who is normally very restless might find the stimulation of being in a reminiscence group sufficient to enable them to reduce, or even stop wandering while the group is going on.

Practical considerations

Finding a suitable meeting place for the group is important. It needs to be accessible, reasonably quiet and private. Creating a warm, comfortable safe environment will go a long way towards helping to ensure a group's success. Basic catering facilities are a great advantage, as are spaces where practical activities which might create some mess can be undertaken. Easy access to a garden area or park will extend the possibilities of the project. Leaders need to think about how to arrange the seating and necessary tables, including creating areas within the main space where smaller groups can talk more intimately. Appropriate space needs to be found to display the resources and triggers during the meetings, and to store them between meetings.

An evocation by Catherine Goor of the Belgian RYCT group's apartment in Brussels and its impact on the project participants

"This Tuesday the sky is grey. A few raindrops tell me I must cover up. But the sun shines in my heart. What impatience to find very soon all my friends in this little apartment at 114 Soldier Street, situated in the middle of Brussels near the huge Basilica of Koekelberg. It is a flat on the first floor where we meet every week above a kitchen shop. (We are not at all like an institution!)

At last I am there. I walk up a few stairs and already I can smell the delicious odour of the coffee. It's very warm and friendly. How great it is to be here!

The photographs taken last week are stuck on the mirror. They put me straight into the atmosphere. Little by little, the others arrive. We kiss and we remember that we know each other. "Hello Claire" "Hello. It's lovely here. Just like home... know you, don't I!"

The comfortable settees invite us to sit and enjoy the meeting.

"Welcome to all. I'm happy to see you."

Above, I have described the reaction of Gaston, a caree with recently developed dementia who was a member of our group. Through the rhythm and the mood of the sessions, he showed us that he was able to have a clear memory of the previous sessions.

After we kissed hello, he could feel an atmosphere he already knew. Five minutes after he arrived, everybody was comfortably installed. On the coffee table in the middle of the room, cups and coffee, just like two weeks earlier. Suddenly he turned to his right, put his hand on Ferdy's shoulder and with a beautiful smile said, "I'm so happy to see you again."

When we have asked the carees and carers what they thought about the meetings they told us that they all loved the intimacy of the apartment.

Claire: Here we can laugh and have fun, just like at home.

Gaston: These sessions are the best moments for me.

Helen: (his wife) I see in this place in these sessions help for isolated families who are also psychologically distressed. The doctor is there for my husband but I feel lonely and I also need understanding, comforting as well as the rest of the family. I see this apartment as a refuge where I can rebuild myself to face the new personality of my husband and to make stronger my own personality."

Ferdy: (a caree) I come here to replace the holes in my reservoir of memories.

Conclusion

The apartment gave birth to intimacy, friendship and also gave a chance to everyone to take his place with a large space to communicate and to be listened to. Everyone knows that this is right. This apartment is a place which makes it easier for everyone to be equal. No carers, no carees, no leaders... just friends.

A flat was rented for the duration of the project. It was furnished with second hand furniture, bought or borrowed, and filled with many objects which acted as potent triggers for participants. Workers and volunteers worked hard to create a comfortable homely environment where group members felt safe and had a good time. (Belgium)

Pre-project visits

Whatever type of group or project is planned, it is a good idea, if possible, to visit the home of each participant before the group begins to meet. The information gathered on this visit will help make sure that what is offered is tailored to the needs of every group member.

It also allows those people who are going to be involved in running group sessions to introduce themselves to each participant, and to answer any questions they may have about the project.

As well as basic information such as the age, family background and important relationships of participants, these visits will give an opportunity to find out a little about their working lives, and their interests, current and past.

Home visits will also give the group leader or volunteer insight into the day-to-day difficulties faced by carers. It can highlight the opportunities the home environment offers for reminiscence resources (for example photos, objects, certificates) and home-based reminiscence activities which could complement those undertaken in the group.

Wherever possible, it is desirable for two people to visit so that one can speak with the person with dementia and the other with the family carer.

However, where this is the case, it is also desirable to bring them together later in the same visit to fill in the background on their shared lives so that they enter the project on as equal a basis as possible.

This approach was successfully used in the Oslo and Copenhagen RYCT projects. The Oslo volunteers visited the people with dementia regularly after the initial visit, taking care of them during the *'carers-only'* sessions of the project.

Not everyone is comfortable about using or hearing terms such as 'dementia' or 'Alzheimer's disease'. It is a good idea to think about what terms to use within a project and on visits to group members in their own homes.

If you think members may be uncomfortable about specific terms it may be better to start off by talking about 'memory difficulties.' It is best to listen to how each person talks about their disabilities and use their words where possible.

Carers enjoy trying out some of the reminiscence activities themselves in a carers-only group. (Vienna)

The Life of a Group

Early Meetings

If you are planning to follow the RYCT model, the following section will help you to prepare family carers and others involved in the project. If you are not involving family carers but are setting up a reminiscence group for people with dementia, you will still need to prepare all those involved. (See the section on preparing volunteers and group helpers on pages 53.)

Preparing the family carers

During the first meetings, group members need time to get to know one another and to establish trust. Some carers in the group may have been isolated for some time and will have an overwhelming need to share their experiences with others.

> **"In our group an egg-timer was used to help carers limit the time spent talking about their daily lives as carers, and allow the group to move on to reminiscence activities."**
>
> **(Amsterdam)**

Leaders need to recognise this and plan the structure of early meetings accordingly. However, a reminiscence group is not primarily a *'support group'* as usually understood and the process of reminiscing itself will both help members to get to know one another, and assist carers to feel listened to and appreciated.

It is important therefore that even early meetings set the tone for the forthcoming project. While allowing some time for carers to talk about their difficulties, setting limits to this will ensure that there is also time for introducing reminiscence and the tools which will allow them to do this well with people with dementia.

Perhaps the most important purpose of the early meetings is to introduce the idea that reminiscence can be helpful to carers. The easiest way to do this is to allow carers themselves time to practice and enjoy reminiscence. In this way, they will experience the value of being listened to and the pleasure of telling others stories about their lives. Throughout the project, time will need to be set aside for carers to do this, and it is likely to be much appreciated as carers often feel engulfed by their situation and feel they have little time for themselves.

Carers' comments

"I'm so grateful to be able to share experiences with such lovely people and although we don't talk about what's going on in our own lives now, we do enjoy talking about what we used to do." **(London)**

"I have learned a great deal that makes it easier to cope in everyday life. I have felt social support and understanding. We are not so alone with our problems anymore". **(Oslo)**

"I see it as a positive experience to meet others affected and exchange views. The friendly and positive spirit of our meetings makes them a social occasion which eases the loneliness, apart from anything else. Participation gives me relaxation and consolation as well as practical advice." **(Finland)**

"This is different from the usual support group which tends to focus on negative aspects of caring. In those meetings you end up talking about the person you are caring for - this group is entirely different. Here you are talking about yourself and your partner." **(Bradford)**

"The project gives me more understanding about life with dementia. I find it easier to cope with my person now. Communication is better, and I have the feeling I am not alone." **(Vienna)**

"Sharing memories with my wife as a result of the project has been the first time we have talked at the same level for many years." **(Amsterdam)**

"I really enjoy watching my mother speak with other people. She will respond, co-operate and take part in such a lively way, and she doesn't need to fight them." **(London)**

"I have never known how my mother lived until now. I realise I should have found out much sooner and now I shall start to tell my children." **(Stockholm)**

"Earlier I did not know anything about reminiscence. I am happy to do something for my husband. It is a big task to learn how to communicate with a person with dementia. I need to try new ways to do it all the time." **(Copenhagen)**

However the second purpose of these early meetings is to introduce and develop skills which will enable carers to stimulate and listen to the memories of those they care for, the people with dementia. Adopting the role of listener will not be easy for some carers, but exercises which help them to understand how uncomfortable it feels not to be listened to, and how pleasurable it is when somebody really does pay attention to what they say, will help them to recognise the value of listening to the person with dementia.

The pleasure of being listened to attentively in a comfortable environment (Brussels)

Some carers who are very tired and perhaps unwell may not be able to listen. If leaders can recognise this, they may be able to suggest other ideas which will be more likely to succeed. For example, they might suggest that carers invite a neighbour or relative to become involved in reminiscence work at home, providing stimulation and being willing to listen.

Also some people just are not good listeners, but they can often find other ways of practising reminiscence with the person with dementia, for example by taking the person they care for on visits to places which were important to them in the past.

In these early sessions, carers can be helped to think about how they communicate with their person with dementia and to explore alternative approaches.

For example, if we give the experience in an exercise of what it feels like to be interrupted in the middle of a story because something may be slightly incorrect, we can help the carer to understand how easy it is to lose the thread and also lose focus and confidence. Similarly if we show what it feels like to be talked about as if you are not there, or to have someone speak for you, it will help carers to have more sympathy with how the person with dementia may feel and explore other ways of responding.

Family carers are often very sensitive to the gap between what their person used to be able to do and their present capabilities. While the rest of a group is delighted by what he says or does, his wife may think 'but a few years ago he was touring the world lecturing to audiences of 100'. This thought may be reflected in her body language, and give him very different cues. Participating in a reminiscence project will raise carers' awareness of the subtle but important messages they may be inadvertently sending to the person they care for.

Danny, in his prime, regales his colleagues with an after-dinner speech. Today he has difficulty in making himself understood at all, a situation that his family finds difficult to adjust to. (London)

Preparing the volunteers and group helpers

During the early meetings volunteers and helpers will also be getting to know each other. They will be beginning to understand the pleasure and value of reminiscing by enjoying and sharing their own memories. They will be developing the skills needed to do good reminiscence work with people with memory difficulties.

They need to learn how to listen attentively, and not rush people who may need time and encouragement to begin reminiscing. They need to learn how to ask questions without testing and how to develop stories in different ways.

During these first meetings leaders will also want to establish the ethos of the project, aiming to create a space where everybody has an enjoyable time, and feels safe and valued. Talking about ground-rules for group behaviour is a good starting point, but just as important will be the way leaders and volunteers behave towards one another and the participants.

Encouraging a special atmosphere will help to ensure that just attending the group gives members a boost each week. One of the tasks of the group will be to find ways to trigger responses in the people with dementia and inspire them to participate and feel good about expressing themselves.

Different ways of learning

Leaders will need to explore different ways of working with carers to find the best way to help them think about how they relate to the people they care for, and how they can develop better ways of coping. Some older people who are not used to training exercises may learn more from positive role models offered by other carers in the group.

A carer who is coping well can share their ideas and offer practical suggestions to other carers. Leaders can make time for this sort of positive modelling, while intervening to prevent or minimise reinforcement of negative attitudes.

"M. spontaneously made a speech, thanking us for our work. His wife initially found this embarrassing but was later encouraged by the group's positive reaction"

Group leader, Finland

Ground Rules

It is important to talk early in the life of the group about what being in that group means for individual members. This includes discussing their expectations and agreeing how people should behave towards one another. Ground rules are the resulting agreements made between members of the group after such discussions. The agreements they make can be discussed, changed or amended by the group at any time.

Suggested issues

Confidentiality

Are participants happy for things said in meetings to be discussed outside the group?

Respecting differences

It is possible that participants turn out to have very different views and opinions about past and present. An agreement to take a non-judgmental attitude to people who are different may save trouble later on.

The importance of the people with dementia

The project is for the people with dementia as much as it is for everyone else. An agreement that the most important thing is for them to feel accepted and supported (regardless of whether they participate successfully in any reminiscence activities) may be a good idea.

Giving equal concern to each person's needs

Everyone needs a chance to talk, and to receive a share of the group's attention. An agreement that this is the case may help 'big talkers' allow others to take their turn.

Expressing feelings

Old memories can bring up strong feelings. An agreement that expressing feelings is acceptable and welcome in this group can help people to feel all right if they are overcome by emotion.

Acceptance of evaluation

Participants need to accept that there will be evaluation and possibly subsequent writing about the project and to be reassured that their anonymity will be safeguarded if this is what they need.

Looking at case-studies is another way of allowing carers to observe others in a similar situation and reflect on how well or badly they are coping. If this type of approach is used it is important that leaders avoid moralising and allow carers to come to their own conclusions in a supportive and positive atmosphere.

(See the example from Denmark below.)

Learning can be reinforced for some people by taking material home. Handouts for carers were developed by the Network Partners in each country on reminiscence, forgetfulness and listening but leaders may also develop their own materials for carers.

An Example from Denmark

At our second meeting we saw a Danish TV programme, showing the everyday life of a person with severe dementia and his carer.

The first scene shows the carer trying to train the person with dementia to read, using a reading-book from the very first class in school! She is doing this because the doctor had told her to train her husband, so that no more brain cells would die. He is not able to read and is obviously uncomfortable with the situation.

The next scene shows her sending him into the dining-room with a plate. When he comes into the room, he has forgotten why he is there and why he has got a plate in his hand, so he goes back to her in the kitchen, where she scolds him.

As a contrast, another scene shows her dusting. She gives him a cloth and they go beside one another and are doing the work together.

A fourth scene shows the home-help asking him questions about the use of an object. He is not able to tell her (he has difficulty communicating verbally) but his hands are showing how the thing was used. The home-help doesn't see this and tells him the use of the object.

A fifth scene shows the couple watching a cine film together. The film was taken when they were a young couple and had small children. For the first and only time in the programme, we see him engaged and smiling.

After watching these extracts the carers' first response was, *"This is exactly like me - this is what I do, I scold, etc . .."*.

Seeing a video about another carer with whom they could identify, gave the Danish carers new awareness and understanding. It helped them to see some of the difficulties faced by carers and people with dementia, both in terms of communication and feelings. It also helped them to reflect on their own behaviour. (Copenhagen)

Sharing memories of working life (Copenhagen)

Learning about reminiscence

When reminiscing, we select what we share with others. Whatever a person says needs to be accepted as true by the listener. Each person's memories are unique and may be different from those of others who experience the same event (brothers and sisters for instance).

The truth may be embellished, and over time some memories may merge with others. Although people with dementia have trouble remembering things and get facts and times *'wrong'*, their memories are just as important and *'true'* for them.

This may be easier in theory than in practice. For instance, a new listener can listen to a story, and accept it as truth. It is much more difficult for a carer to respond in a positive way to a story (perhaps of a shared experience) which is completely *'wrong'*.

Opportunities for carers to tell their own stories can help them to accept the *'inaccurate'* memories of the person with dementia as part of their disabilities. If carers can learn to do this they can begin to see these stories as a successful attempt to communicate and may then be able to enjoy them with the person with dementia.

(Refer back to the section on dementia for further information.)

Old matchbox labels bring back memories. (Finland)

> **❝Reminiscence encouraged family interaction which was closer to normal. The simple pleasure of recognising a familiar object or recalling a forgotten melody were rays of sunshine in the fog of forgetfulness, and perhaps the feeling of pleasure enhanced their lives briefly, even if the reason for it was instantly forgotten.❞**
>
> **Group leader, Finland**

Outline session plans developed for the RYCT project

Four outline session plans follow, to help prepare carers and helpers for reminiscence work with people with dementia. These may be adapted as some groups may not be able to hold four meetings.

It is important that carers and helpers have some time to learn the basics and practice reminiscence themselves before starting the group work with people with dementia. Whatever leaders decide to do they need to give carers the opportunity to learn about active listening and communication as well as some time to talk about their situation as carers.

Session 1: Introductions

Objectives
The overall objective is to encourage participation - this is everyone's first session. It should make the participants feel that they want to keep coming. It should feel welcoming, safe, fun, and interesting. The main purposes of the session are:
- to introduce the project ● to introduce people to each other
- to generate enthusiasm ● to reduce anxiety
- to introduce the functions of reminiscence.

Opening round
Introduce the leaders and helpers and explain a little about what the project or group is going to be doing. Go round the group allowing each participant to spend a few minutes introducing themselves. This may be the first time that some carers will have been able to speak to others about their situation as a carer, so readers must be flexible about the time allowed during the first meeting, and let carers know that a little time will be reserved in future meetings for this to happen.

Learning about reminiscence and discovering how it feels to explore the past
Work in pairs and spend a few minutes talking to your partner about your schooldays. One person in each pair should talk to the other for 2 or 3 minutes. Then that person should listen while the other talks for a few minutes. They listen carefully to each other.

Possible prompts
(A list of words to help bring back memories may be given out on sheets or written on a board) School buildings, teachers, school dinners, the toilets, the playground, reward and punishments, school friends, favourite and worst subjects.

Discussion
Discuss in the full group what happened and how it felt? The leader should relate the points made in the discussion to the value of reminiscence.

During the week
Ask participants to look out for a memory from the past during the coming week. Also ask them to see if the person with dementia mentions anything from the past and make a note of it.

Closing activity:
Ask each participant to say in one sentence what s/he hopes to gain from the project.

The carers practice communicating back to back without being able to see their partner's face or actions. (Oslo)

Session 2: The gift of listening

Objectives
- to continue group building, reducing anxiety and generating enthusiasm
- introduction to the value of good listening, the discomfort of inattention

Opening round
Ask each person to report back on how their week went, and any memories they and their person recalled. Some limits may need to be set to this so that time is left to do the listening exercises.

Experiencing the discomfort of inattention
Pair up with a different person to last week's partner. Listen to your partner telling you what they did last Sunday, but only really pay attention to them for the first half minute or so. After that time allow your attention to wander. Then swap over. The whole exercise shouldn't last more than about two or three minutes. Ask people to talk about what happened and how they felt. Some people find this exercise very difficult as they do not wish to be impolite or to let it be thought that they are sometimes 'bad listeners'. However, if even a few people are willing to try the exercise, it is worthwhile as it gives a very direct experience of what it feels like not to be listened to and is an effective 'raiser of consciousness'.

Comparing the experience of full attention
In the same pairs, give your full attention to your partner's account of Sundays in childhood, 3 minutes each way. Remind people to listen to each other for the full 3 minutes. Suggest possible prompts: clothes, food, rituals, religion, activities, visits to relatives, etc.

Exploring how it feels when someone speaks for us
Join with another pair. Each person tells the group about their partner's childhood Sundays. Allow no more than 3 minutes each. Talk about how this felt and then discuss the different experiences of all three exercises.
Discuss:

the value of good listening
the importance of listening to people with dementia
how it feels when others speak for you.

During the week
Ask participants to remember something from their childhood and talk to the person with dementia about it.

Closing activity
Ask participants if they can suggest a favourite song from when they were young, and sing one or two of these as a group.

Session 3: Coping with incomplete and unconventional communication

Objectives
- to continue group building, supporting and generating enthusiasm
- to experience the frustrations of incomplete communication
- to reflect on how much effort it takes to achieve understanding
- to put forward the view that it is worth trying to understand because people with dementia are trying to communicate, and it does make a difference to them when we listen
- to think about the use of metaphors and symbols in communication, particularly with respect to communicating feelings.

Opening round
Allow each person to talk very briefly about their week, and to share any memories of childhood they had with their person during the week.

Experiencing communication with words, but without non-verbal signals
Choose a partner. Sit back to back, not touching. Then give your partner a set of directions e.g. from your house to the station, shops, park etc. Then swap over.

Exercise to experience communication without words
Give your partner a message without words. e.g. my car has broken down, a wish for particular food, a desire to visit relatives.

Experiencing trying to communicate with few words, and trying to understand someone else who cannot say much.
Join up with another pair to work in fours. Each person in turn tells the other three something about a special occasion using only four words (repeated as often as you like) and any sounds and gestures that you like. The listeners have to guess what you are telling them about.

Discussion
Relate what people have just done to the experience of people with dementia, and for those who are trying to communicate with them. Hand out and read one of John Killick's poems (see page 18). Think about what the poem might mean and share different interpretations. Discuss how difficult it is sometimes to work out what someone is trying to communicate and what this must be like for someone with dementia. Note that people with dementia sometimes use language imaginatively and symbolically.

During the week
Ask people to look out for occasions when they have difficulty working out what their person is trying to communicate. Notice moments when the person with dementia does not seem to understand what their carer, or someone else, is trying to say to them.

Closing activity
Read a couple of popular nonsense poems and enjoy them together ('The owl and the pussy cat', or other Edward Lear or Lewis Carroll poems)

Session 4: Enabling and recording reminiscence

Objectives
- to continue group building, reducing anxiety and generating enthusiasm
- to introduce planned reminiscence
- to explain the use of multi-sensory triggers
- to experience the satisfaction of recording
- to consider the uses of recorded material for people with dementia

Opening Round
Spend a few minutes talking about the week, and sharing experiences about moments when carers didn't understand what their person was trying to communicate or didn't understand what the carer was saying to them.

Experiencing planned reminiscence, using multi-sensory triggers
Working as a whole group, pass some objects around which will trigger memories of childhood toys, games and activities, for example a skipping rope, teddy, ball, marbles, cricket bat. Encourage everyone to say something.

Experiencing making a record of memories
Encourage everyone to make a record of their memory in some way. Suggest: writing a letter to a grandchild, writing a postcard to an old friend , using members of the group to illustrate the memory and taking a photo, draw a plan of the street or playground, write down the rules of a game or tape a song. People might like to work in twos or threes to help each other to get started. Direct people to resource material on different modes of recording. Then make a spontaneous and informal exhibition of the recorded reminiscence material.

Discuss how they felt about sharing their memories, and how they felt handling the triggers. Talk about how to encourage memories without asking direct questions.

Planning for the first joint session.
Inform participants about the topic for your first joint meeting and discuss as a group:
> how to make the people with dementia feel at ease,
> for instance what refreshments to have,
> whether people may want to smoke and where this might happen,
> what each carer might bring to trigger memories about the theme you have chosen.

During the week
Look for objects or photos which might trigger memories for the person with dementia about the theme. Encourage their involvement in this search and spend some time enjoying any objects you find with them.

Closing activity
Select some children's songs or nursery rhymes and sing or recite them together.

Preparing and structuring reminiscence sessions

Leaders will need to set aside time each week to think about and prepare for the next meeting. Appropriate resources need to be gathered and activities will need to be planned. Involving other members of the group in this planning and resourcing will help everyone to feel part of the project. It will also ensure that responsibility is shared and all members feel that they are equal partners in the group. Each group member needs to find and develop a role which suits them. This might involve helping to set up the room, organising refreshments for a session, locating appropriate triggers around a theme, or taking responsibility for one group member during the sessions or keeping in contact with that person between sessions.

The reason for the meetings is to do reminiscence and a useful way to maintain the interest of all group participants is to involve them in planning each session and encourage everyone to look out suitable objects, pictures, and other triggers to get the discussion off to a good start. The people with dementia can be involved with this, although, of course, they may need a lot of reminders.

The meeting room in a sheltered housing unit's lounge is filled with objects brought by RYCT workers and carers involved in the project. (Bradford)

The meetings that people with dementia attend will be based around a theme and leaders will need to plan them. Carers can then also be involved in preparing for sessions by looking out for suitable objects, pictures and other triggers from home or from the local area. With encouragement and support people with dementia will enjoy participating in this search, which in itself can be a pleasurable activity.

Each session ends with relaxation movements bowing and waving and saying "Good-bye until next time" (Amsterdam)

The length of meetings may need to be adapted to suit the individual needs of participants. However you may find that some people with dementia who are normally very restless or have a short attention span, may, once they have settled in a group, be able to concentrate and enjoy a session for much longer than carers would have thought possible. During the early meetings, if carers are worried about this, it might be helpful to reassure them by letting them know that they can leave early if their person is uncomfortable or finding the session difficult.

Security and a sense of belonging are fostered by having a certain amount of ritual in the meetings. Things such as singing the same song at the start or finish of meetings, playing a game together every session or sharing food and drink, gives a predictable structure which is reassuring and promotes a sense of familiarity. These rituals need to be reviewed to make sure that they are enjoyable and meaningful, so that they do not become routine, and a limiting factor.

Whether or not carers are involved, it is very important to have enough support to enable people with dementia to have individual attention where necessary. In normal social situations people with dementia often feel left out or left behind. We need to reserve a special place at the centre of activities for the participants with dementia. To make sure that people with dementia have a chance to express themselves they need to feel safe. They need extra time and space to be able to contribute and should never feel rushed.

The group needs to be a place with a good positive atmosphere where exciting things happen and where people share stories and experiences in interesting ways. This atmosphere is made from things like a warm welcome, food and drink, music, conversation and enjoyable activities. It is also essential that people feel supported and understood, and that this applies equally to people with dementia and their carers. There may often be compelling reasons why participants do not come to meetings and it is important that leaders make contact when people don't turn up, and take an interest in what is happening in people's lives outside the group.

Making a homely atmosphere was crucial to the project's success. (Brussels)

For many people with dementia and their carers, life lacks opportunities for social interaction. The group needs to provide these opportunities. The group leader needs to organise things so that people enjoy one another's company and to ensure that new relationships can grow. This can be done, for example, by planning who sits together, and by moving people for different activities.

It is important for group leaders to be alert to what is happening in the group and flexible about the direction it takes. If one idea seems to be falling flat, be prepared to move on and try something else. If a leader's attitude and the environment are right, all sorts of creative activities can be tried on the basis that some will work and others will not. It would be a mistake to jettison ideas which do not work immediately. They may work on another occasion when the group is in a different mood.

Dealing with painful memories

> **"Tivea told the group:"The cossacks used to invade villages and towns in Roumania and violated young girls. We had been told to leave the town by night and walked 30km arriving at 5am at a place where we were hidden by other people. Later we went back safely to our town. I think I never told this story before, maybe once, to my daughter."**
>
> **Paris**

Both carers and people with dementia are dealing with loss and change in their lives, and it is likely that there will be moments when difficult feelings are expressed or painful memories recalled. Group leaders need to give group members time to get in touch with their feelings before moving on to something else. They must feel that their sadness has been acknowledged and understood. It can be an opportunity for the individual to gain support from the empathy of the group.

> **"A member of the group shared a sad memory referring to the death of a son, describing it very emotionally. Members of the group responded with great empathy. Sharing this moving memory brought the group closer together."**
>
> **Brussels**

> **"One carer admitted, "Easter is a danger to us, we'd rather forget about it, to tell you the truth, because that is when our daughter died." However, the carer did not want the topic changed and decided to attend."**
>
> **Stockholm**

After moments of sadness, sensitivity and good timing are needed so that a positive atmosphere can be restored. This can be done, for instance, by singing an appropriate song, or by gently redirecting attention to a new activity or another person's experience. It is very important that nobody leaves feeling low or exposed. Leaders need to ensure that someone talks to people who have become upset before they go home.

Marie, born in Paris of Polish parents, and her only son join in a discussion group where many people shared troubling memories and found relief. For four out of the eight residents present, a good memory meant only one where they avoided disaster, since their lives had been dominated by the wartime persecution of the Jews. (Paris)

❝At the 9th session I presented a long wooden peg and asked if anyone knew what it was. Some residents recognised it as the thing used to lift wet linen out of the lavoir (collective washing place) in French villages. Some had spent the war in these villages, hiding for safety and the object gave rise to many memories not previously recalled.

Tivea recalled that two military police officers stopped her and asked her her name and she replied "Madame Michel", giving her husband's first name, as the surname would give away the fact that she was Jewish. He asked, "Where are you from?" She wanted to reply, "I am from Central Europe (she is Rumanian) but instead she replied "I am from the Centre." "Well, she is from the Centre!", said one officer to the other, thinking she came from the central part of the same region where people speak with a different accent. This certainly saved her from deportation.

At the end of the session, Tivea spoke to me and said, "Thank you very much, this session has been very enjoyable." I was relieved because I had been worried about how to approach the topic of the war years without causing too much heartbreak.❞

Group leader, Paris

Feedback

After each meeting, if possible, leaders, helpers and volunteers need to feedback on how they feel the meeting went, what worked well, and what if anything failed. Where possible, have a short meeting immediately after each session where workers, volunteers and other helpers can pool information about what they observed in the session while it is fresh in their minds, and share ideas for activities to follow up next time the group meets. Carers often find it helpful to hear from volunteers what their person has been doing and remembering while they were not working together. Encourage volunteers to note down what they noticed in the session.

If you can introduce a structure which enables honest criticism to be made in a positive and supportive way you can encourage the development of a group which works openly and which takes on new ideas for activities and themes as it progresses.

If meetings of this sort are not practical, it is important to devise other ways of gaining feedback and response from everyone involved. Feedback sheets may be given out and filled in by all group members or oral feedback and comments given by telephone or in individual meetings.

Planning for the end of the group

Where a group is running for a limited number of sessions, members need to be prepared for the fact that they they are approaching the end of the project. They should be consulted about how they would like to end it, for example with a party or an outing.

Looking back together over the life of the group and the many activities which have been shared, can help to see the ending in a positive light. Photos and other records of work produced by project members will help the group to review and celebrate the work they have done together.

Some members will be very sad that the group is ending and this feeling needs to be acknowledged. Although the pressure to continue may be strong, it would be a mistake for group leaders to make promises they cannot fulfil regarding further meetings.

However, it may be possible, where group members wish to continue to see each other from time to time, for group leaders to make arrangements for this to happen on a different and more occasional basis, so that friendships can be maintained with some measure of support. There may be a family carer or group helper who may be able to take on this co-ordinating role.

It is necessary to make time before the sessions end to plan for any future contact between group members. If everyone is agreeable, it is a good idea to circulate telephone numbers and addresses to facilitate this. People can then also be informed about one another's birthdays and special anniversaries, but also about illnesses and even deaths occurring after the group has ceased to meet.

Almost all RYCT pilot groups across Europe have continued to meet on an occasional (mostly monthly) basis and in many cases the family carers have expressed willingness to help out with the new RYCT groups which are now forming Carers whose partners or parents have died feel that they want to pass on the reminiscence skills they have acquired and help other carers.

> *It felt to me that the group we had, who had met together continuously over a period of time, had not finished its natural life. I felt the group could do more and the fact that the members have continued to come back proves this. There were strong bonds in the group and it seemed a pity just to chop those off because the project was due to end.*
>
> **Carer, London**

Outings are a means for our group to maintain the valuable social links and friendships made during the project. (Kassel)

Monitoring & Evaluation

Monitoring means recording the information you need to be able report on your project and to look back and learn from experience. This includes recording background information about participants and keeping attendance records with details of the reasons for absence and for dropping out. You will need to have records of session plans, and notes on how the plans worked out in practice. Evaluation can look at many different aspects of a project.

Three important questions are:

● *How well did the project meet its aims and objectives?*
● *What parts of the project were successful and what were not?*
● *In what ways did the project benefit participants?*

You will need a plan which sets out the questions for the evaluation and shows how the information needed to answer them will be gathered. (See right hand column.)

Setting aims and objectives and considering whether they have been met

It is important to set realistic aims, and to think ahead to work out what evidence is needed to prove that they have been met. These aims may have to be adjusted during the life of the project. For example, making sure that everyone speaks may be unrealistic as an aim; given certain people's frailties, it may be more realistic to aim to engage the attention of participants most of the time.

> **"In the RYCT project, social contact and having fun turned out to be one of the most important outcomes for participants although these things had not been included in the original statement of main aims and objectives. They were probably a reason why attendance was so good, and may also have helped carers to be more open to new learning."**
> RYCT evaluator

AIMS, OBJECTIVES & EVIDENCE

Example of an aim, related objectives, and the evidence to show that they have been met.

AIM

To demonstrate the pleasure and value of reminiscence

OBJECTIVE 1

To get people to participate in reminiscence activities

EVIDENCE

[a] Leaders' records of session
[b] Observer reports of sessions
[c] Carers' diary entries
[d] Notes on carers' comments
[e] Attendance records
[f] What people with dementia say and do

OBJECTIVE 2

To enable people to enjoy reminiscence activities

EVIDENCE

[a] Signs of pleasure e.g. smiles, bright eyes
[b] Behaviour changes e.g. going to the toilet less often, staying awake more than usual
[c] Alertness
[d] Helpfulness
[e] Awareness and concern for others
[f] Unexpected ability to remember meetings
[g] Making the effort to communicate

OBJECTIVE 3

To help people to benefit from reminiscence activities as much as possible

EVIDENCE

[a] Carers reporting positive changes
[b] Becoming more communicative
[c] Becoming more confident
[d] More likely to initiate social contact
[e] Changes at home e.g. new activities with the carer, more social contact, accepting a new service

Sample session records from Norwegian RYCT group in Oslo

Session5

This was the first session where people with dementia participated. Two extra volunteers came along to look after the practical details and to give support to the participants. They had helped on the home visits and so were known by members of the group.

- We began by wishing everyone welcome while serving coffee, lemonade and cake. We chatted and sang a few songs. A couple of participants were quiet at first, but began to join in when hearing familiar songs. We talked about childhood memories triggered by singing these songs.

- Carers had been asked to bring an object which might trigger memories for their spouse. Some had brought books describing their past lives. One brought an old Singer sewing machine.

- We looked at the books, giving a lot of attention to the people with dementia, including them without asking direct questions. Even those who were not able to say much seemed to enjoy the positive attention, and became more alert as time went on. One participant, was able to talk at length about the war years, which both she and her husband had written about. She also remembered that they had had a wedding anniversary the day before. We sang the song '*With this ring...*', which she really seemed to appreciate.

- Then we invited members of the group to talk about memories associated with the sewing machine. Many memories were triggered, although sometimes it seemed that the carers tried to 'cover up' for their person or prevent them from having a go. This was probably because they were afraid they would get stuck or not be able to say anything.

- It was exciting watching the carers with those they cared for, though some of them seemed to have trouble accepting their person with dementia's lack of words and unpredictability. It is important to spend some time talking about this at the next meeting.

Task for next session

- Write down something you noticed about your person's reactions at this meeting. Also write down any memories you recall together at home.

Closing Activity

- We ended by singing a hymn often sung at school in the past. Participation in this was not so good as the earlier singing.

Session 6

Opening round:

- *How did you spend the recent Easter holidays?*

- Then we had a round on: *How did your person enjoy the last session?*
  How did you feel about being together with your person here?

- The people with dementia had all enjoyed being in the group. Participants suggested this was probably because we had talked to them and not about them, and not 'above their heads'. All the carers said that they had also enjoyed the session. We talked about the difficult feelings which may come up when the person closest to you behaves oddly. We think it is important to talk openly about this.

- For homework, carers had been asked to notice any memories which came up in the week. They understood objects and photographs could stimulate memories, but were not finding it easy to do this in practice. They probably need more practice in how to help this happen.

- We had asked carers for ideas about singing. They made some suggestions about which songs might be good and felt that cheerful songs were better and more appropriate for our sort of meetings.

- We did the exercise on trying to communicate without words (back to back exercise), then practised using multi sensory triggers by smelling an old bottle of iodine and sharing reminiscences.

- Finally, we looked at an old map from the first world war and talked about memories which were triggered.

Looking at a World War I map in a group session. (Oslo)

Marie-Louise Carrette completes a leader's diary as detailed records are kept of every session. (Brussels)

Record-keeping for monitoring and evaluation

Attendance

Attendance records provide essential evidence of the progress of a project. It is important to keep records of who attends each week, and to find out quickly the reasons for non-attendance. Following up non-attendance is a good way of demonstrating to people with dementia and their carers that they are valued members of the group and that they are missed when they do not attend. When running a project or group of this nature, the leader will need to be prepared to make time to maintain contact with family and other carers between sessions, offering advice and support where necessary.

Observation

An excellent way to see what is happening during a session is to ask a helper or volunteer to observe part or all of a meeting and to record their observations. (See example on facing page) Again it is important that this is done in a positive way so that members do not feel their performance is being judged. The aim of observations of this kind is to gather information about the nature of interactions which happen in a session, and to ensure that all group members are getting the most out of sessions. If you decide to carry out this kind of observation you need to make sure it is done in an unobtrusive way and that note-takers reflect the mood of the group rather than inhibiting it.

An observer may watch and record how a single member of the group responds to the different stimuli and activities during the session, noting degrees of engagement and disengagement and the nature of the person's interactions with others. Alternatively they might attach themselves to a small group and observe what happens within that group. Over a number of weeks, observation of activity and behaviour can give a good indication of how relaxed members are, how engaged they are, and how much they are gaining from the group. These observations might include body language, how often members go to the toilet or out for a smoke, temporary loss of concentration or periods of sleep.

Arthur talks to Alex about his work as a furrier while Chris observes and takes notes, while enjoying the memories with them. (Bradford)

Recording

Keeping a record as you go along is a vital memory aid to help understand what happens in each session. It is best to do this as soon as possible after the session has ended. Recording how each activity went, what was particularly successful and what did not work so well, will help when planning future sessions and perhaps future groups. In addition, recording particular stories and interventions will provide specific examples of the value of the reminiscence sessions for the people with dementia. Often participants in groups are very happy for their experiences to be publicised. A clearance form can be used to get their permission in writing. However, sensitivity must be shown when dealing with wider publicity such as TV and radio and press reports on the project. The confidentiality of what is said in the sessions must be respected and readers should be careful about where information goes. All participants should be asked to respect this.

Extract from observation made by Hannah Zeilig, during a session on entertainment (London)

We moved on to the subject of music, and this seemed much more relevant to Edith. A variety of memories from different periods of her life were stimulated during our conversation, and in no discernable order except that each reminiscence was related to the topic of music: *'I learnt to play the piano when I was younger, I played whatever the teacher wanted me to'* *'We had a gramophone with a big horn.'* In response to me asking what this was like exactly, Edith expressed genuine surprise that I did not know. I fetched paper and coloured pens and asked if she would like to draw one from memory, so that I could see what she meant: *'Now let's think, don't you really know how it was? You had a kind of box and out of that came a horn.'*

Edith drew intently and obligingly clarified what she was doing as she went along, my note taking I explained to her as being necessary so that I could record her memories of how things used to be: *'That is where the record went and it sent the music up to the horn.'*

The delicacy of Edith's drawing was remarkable as was her concentration. She was not prepared to stop sketching until she was satisfied with the result. She was concerned to obtain the right colours for the drawing and filled in the gramophone until the base was completely yellow: *'In those days they were usually brass coloured, they were metal. That is where it comes out and this is where you put the record in. The whole horn was a sort of copper colour I think. It goes round there.'* (See photo, page 91.)

In the meantime, Olive was playing the piano as a background accompaniment to the conversations. This always seems to effectively relax people and gives another focus of conversation, should this be necessary.

Edith, especially, responded positively to the piano music (as indeed, she always does) with her foot tapping and head nodding she continued drawing but with more energy: *'I think that I'll make this a little stronger (referring to the colour of the base). That part really should be more upright, it came up from a stem and widened out. I liked waltzes, and any kind of music, I was nearly always in a choir.'*

We went on to talk about the records that were played on the gramophone, and at this point a volunteer joined us and helped to jog our memories with the names of some old-time singers. The name *'Nelson Eddy'* was recalled and Edith correctly identified him: *'He was a tenor, they were in films with Jeanette MacDonald.'*

Edith was adept at remembering the words to a song called *'Trees'* and was more than happy to interact with other people. She noticed Jim James making loud noises in another part of the room and found this extremely amusing. With the aid of the volunteer, Edith's memory was probed further, we asked her for the titles of songs that she had liked and although these seemed hard to recall, the names of singers and how they sang were easier: *'Jeanette MacDonald, she was a soprano. We know Paul Robeson don't we? Billy Cotton, he had a band, didn't he?'*

Photographs are another way of keeping a record of what happens in a group. This will be useful while the project is running, to remind people of what they did in previous sessions and to build a group history. When the project ends, the photos will prove invaluable to support any written accounts of it or to make a separate exhibition to draw attention to the reminisence activity for other interested people.

A video recording of the sessions will yield all sorts of information regarding the level of participation of individuals, types of interaction, non-verbal communication, special relationships, progress of individuals and the whole group. A video recording of a session in its entirety will give an objective record, although it obviously cannot record every interaction. It will give insights for leaders and other helpers regarding their styles of working and, when sensitively used, this material can prove to be an invaluable teaching aid. There should be a clear understanding between the group leader and the videomaker as to what is to be filmed and for what purpose. Again, the agreement of the group members to the presence of a camera should be sought at the outset. Where video footage is of particularly high quality, it may constitute a useful promotional tool for the group's work and for reminiscence as a worthwhile activity.

Carers' Diaries

If carers are involved, then asking them to keep a reminiscence diary can be a useful means of recording their response to what happens in the sessions and how they have used opportunities for reminiscence between sessions. Some carers will be happy to keep this kind of record, while others will find it very difficult. It should never be made into a punishing homework and should certainly not be compulsory.

These diaries can be particularly helpful if there is an opportunity for carers to feed back to the other carers and the group leader and to share in successes and difficulties. If the diary entries are looseleaf, they can be photocopied by the group leader and the originals returned to the carer.

Assessing the benefits of the project to participants

It is not easy to prove that a project has been of lasting benefit to participants. Dementia generally gets worse with time, and a reminiscence project cannot be expected to improve a person's memory, nor magically make caring run smoothly. There may be considerable changes to participants' lives during the life of a project - e.g. a period of decline, adjustment to a new service.

This makes it unlikely that simple *'before and after'* measures will reflect only the impact of the project and not other developments in people's lives. It is not easy to find standard tests that will demonstrate a significant change in either carers or people with dementia following a project. However post-project feedback sheets and follow-up interviews can give rich qualitative information about participants' feelings about being involved, both positive and negative.

After the project has ended

Where possible, a post-project interview with participants can be useful, allowing them to feed back whether they found the project enjoyable and helpful, and what they felt were the high and low points.

A useful exercise is to review all the sources of information about the impact of the project, and then write a brief summarising paragraph or two to indicate what has been accomplished. **Such a summary could become a useful means for influencing the opinions of people who hold resources, senior managers and others, whose support will be essential if such projects are to continue in the future.**

A Stockholm Carer's Diary entry

In the group we talked about our first jobs, wages etc. Looked at some objects: hairdressing stuff and an old-fashioned typewriter among other things.

Mother told about her early working experiences, but not with the same ease, finding the words and memories as when we were on our own a few days earlier. Mother seemed restrained by talking in front of so many people, I think, but she liked it. Nice for me to watch mother when she turned the curling tongs showing how to make it cooler. She still knew the way!

When we talked about these matters at home, Mother remembered very well (only with some trouble finding the words), but she got sad when I asked her what she had done with her first wages. I asked her what the matter was and Mother said: 'Don't tell me my mother is gone .... she isn't is she?' After that we talked mostly about Granny. Finally Mother recalled she was dead (but she knew all the time, because she was sad). Mother thought it was odd that she couldn't remember her (Granny's) funeral. But when I described it for her and Granny had been at the Ersta Hospital, she remembered some things around it. Suddenly she mentioned some other people and said that they were also dead (which is true). 'Almost all are gone, everybody one used to know, it is so sad' Mother said. She was moved and upset, but she wanted to talk about this.

A Bradford Carers diary page

Tom went to Woodward Court Day Centre for the first time last Friday, he seemed to have enjoyed the day. I must say that I am glad it went so well. We hope that this may be the first of many visits (meeting new people, going for outings can only be a good thing).

This week when polishing the dining table, Tom said he remembered that the table had belonged to his mum, having the family meals at the table. This also brought forth the memory that his mum had died at middle age. This left me with very mixed feelings, because Tom had loved his mum dearly, yet I was glad he could still recall those memories.

"According to her carer, Winifred remembered nothing about the project and could not say what had happened after the particular sessions. However, when she arrived for a reunion session, six months after the project had ended, she clearly had expectations that she would have a good time and that she would be able to relax with friends. This showed us that we must keep an open mind as to how much people with dementia are holding on to the good experiences they have and retain strong associations which they cannot put into words."

Bradford

Winifred enjoys the session with Doreen, a volunteer, whom she has got to know during the months of the project. (Bradford)

Summary of conclusions of RYCT Evaluators' report

The Remembering Yesterday Caring Today approach offered new, positive, enjoyable ways to communicate and to discover or rediscover shared mutual enjoyment.

There is ample evidence to show that people with dementia were stimulated to communicate, in conversation and also through music, drama, d drawing and other activities. In addition, much communication took place and was enjoyed between carers, volunteers and leaders.

Reminiscence was successfully introduced to people, and valued by them.

Carers started with very different attitudes and coping styles, and some were already taking a positive approach to dementia. Many felt better about the way they were coping after the project, and some were also able to achieve changes in behaviour.

There is a large body of evidence showing that there were high levels of enjoyment among participants, and important social gains. It was not just carers and people with dementia who enjoyed the project. Leaders and volunteers also found it enjoyable, and an 'eye-opener' regarding the lived experience of dementia.

We believe that the RYCT approach has much to offer people, both as a training experience, and as an antidote to burn-out among dementia care professionals.

The cross-country findings despite contextual and regional differences, were very similar. Differences in income and social status, education, gender and relationships, although needing to be sensitively addressed as part of the work, did not prove to be barriers to shared engagement.

The nature of relationships between carer and person with dementia, and other factors, influenced how quickly carers were able to concentrate on and benefit from their own meeting s and feel comfortable in leaving those they were responsible for in the care of others.

These factors also affected the people with dementia, and there was some evidence that they benefited most when they were involved to the same extent as their carers.

There is evidence that the project was valuable in the day care context, facilitating links between service user and home, and enabling both carers and people with dementia to become more positive about day care. However, accepting services is one of the milestones in adjusting to dementia, and we feel that RYCT is particularly valuable to people not yet using services.

The encouraging outcomes from this project suggest that the RYCT approach should become widely accessible to people responsible for dementia services.

Reminiscence Themes

This section offers a range of reminiscence themes and related activities. The emphasis is on creative and practical exploration of key areas of the lives of the participants; the aim is that everyone will be able to contribute their own memories. The reminiscence activities are intended to provide opportunities for exchange and social interaction around shared experience. Each session should be seen as an enjoyable occasion for talk and action in the present.

We need to find as many accessible forms of exchange as possible so that everyone can participate and there is a failure-free ethos. Quirky or bizarre contributions will be offered confidently if people feel that they are likely to be acceptable and if the group feels like a safe and interesting place to be. **Humour is essential!**

The people with dementia should always be at the centre of the meetings. All those involved need to work together to make sure that the voices of the people with dementia are heard and that they have a good time.

One of the benefits of reminiscence is that it can create a social occasion for everyone involved, including professional and family carers and volunteers. Where family carers are involved, there will be the added benefit of seeing the person they care for having fun and relating successfully with others.

It is also important to consider the needs of each individual member when planning a group session so that individual activities and support can be arranged where necessary.

May enjoys being the centre of attention with her daughter Pat and Eileen, a volunteer, listening to her memories. (London)

> **Tom found group activities very difficult. He was nervous and could not communicate easily. Leaders found that he could relax and enjoy a session if the same volunteer sat with him each week and brought specific materials and triggers which fitted in with his interests and abilities. As he became more relaxed and confident, Tom was able to participate in some of the group activities but continued to benefit from one-to-one attention from the volunteer.**
> Bradford

Each theme includes ideas for activities which can be used to begin a session, suggested triggers, exercises and activities.

Suggestions are also offered of ways in which carers can continue activities around the theme outside the group. In many cases themes will overlap so that for instance in talking about *'Where I grew up'* members may begin discussing *'Schooldays'*.

The ideas for activities should be seen as examples and suggestions, not exclusive of other ways to explore the topic. In sessions involving people with dementia, leaders and helpers will need to have the flexibility to try a number of different ideas and see what triggers memories and enjoyment.

Some of the ideas suggested may seem ambitious, but they may well work if the person with dementia is feeling relaxed and has enough memories of the particular topic. Sometimes persevering with a trigger can produce a response, where initially there seems to be no recognition. This is the often case regardless of whether the trigger is being offered in the group situation or at home, as people's current mood is bound to have an effect on their level of receptivity.

> *"I showed my mother a pair of curling tongs which, at first, evoked the response that they were "a fork, something to eat with."*
>
> *At the time, I was standing by her bed and she was looking up at me. The next time I showed them to her, I was kneeling and she was sitting on the bed.*
>
> *I said that I had found them and wondered what they were.*
> *She replied, "They are for your hair", and she showed me how to use them."*
>
> **Carer, London**

Another reason for including a wide variety of ideas is that some may be used to stimulate discussion and activities in groups where carers sometimes meet separately from the people with dementia. In these groups, carers can try out a range of activities and then begin to explore the theme at home and assemble suitable triggers before the next meeting involving the people with dementia.

The suggested themes were chosen as, taken together, they cover the lifespan of the participants from early childhood through to early adult life. However there are a great many more themes which provide an excellent basis for reminiscence sessions and which may give pleasure and stimulus to a group. Some themes which we have not included, but which have been tried and found successful by groups in the RYCT project are the war years, Sundays, health and sickness, setting up home, hobbies, gardens and gardening.

Although we have not included a separate theme for the war years, most older people lived through the Second World War, and have many memories of that time. Because some of these memories may be difficult and painful, care needs to be taken when introducing this topic.

Most groups in the RYCT project did not have a separate session devoted to the war years, although memories of that time did come out, for instance, when talking about courtship and marriage as many of the participants met and married during or after the war. Other sadder memories emerged as trust within the groups built up. Even those who had experienced real trauma were able and wanted to share their memories of that time. (See page 59 on painful memories.)

Father in uniform, 1916 (Kassel)

MY CHILDHOOD HOME AND FAMILY

This is a very rich subject, and one which often provides lots of memories for people with dementia. Among the topics which might be covered within this theme are:

- family members
- favourite foods and mealtimes
- games
- bedtimes
- being naughty and being punished
- childhood illnesses
- household chores
- bathtimes.

A selection of ideas for activities are set out below, and members can explore a number of these, and develop those that are most successful in triggering memories or enjoyment.

TRIGGERS

Family photos, Bible, candle in holder, stone hot water bottle, chamber pot, scrubbing brush, bar soap, menthol crystals, cough linctus, toys, any personal objects relating to childhood brought in by participants.

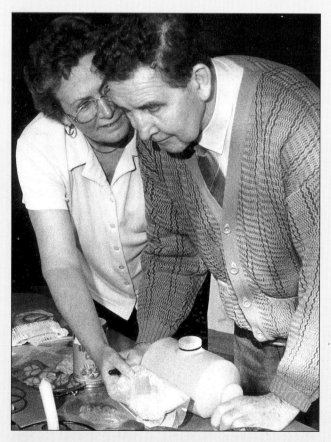

Jim's memories are triggered by objects recalled from childhood. (London)

It is important to take into account the age of participants when selecting triggers. A candle or stone hot-water bottle for instance may not evoke memories for participants in their fifties/sixties.

STARTERS

- The session might begin with some familiar songs from early childhood. Leaders may have some ideas but may also invite requests or suggestions from group members. Although not everyone will remember all the words, this can be a group effort, and some people will be happy to hum, whistle or tap out the rhythm.
- Ask members of the group to show any photos they have found of themselves when younger, noting details of dress/setting and the state of the photo.
- If there are other people in the photo, can they be identified?
- Some people may bring photos of their parents or even grandparents and these should also be circulated. If some people do not have a photo, you may be able to approach relatives for help.

> Look out for differences as well as shared experience. These too can be points of interest and can make individuals and the group feel special. For example a group member may have grown up in another country or come from a different social class, but this should be respected and enjoyed by the group.

ACTIVITIES

'A PHOTOMONTAGE OF CHILDHOOD'
MAKING AN EXHIBITION

- Making a small exhibition from the photos can be a useful way of creating a feeling of being a group. This can be as small an exercise as pinning the photos to a display board by placing drawing pins round the outside of the photos, being careful not to damage the original, or by enlarging the images on a photocopier, or scanner.

- When you look at the photographs as a group you may well find that connections are made and memories are evoked by other people's photographs. The detail which is revealed by enlarging can help to retrieve more memories for the person whose photograph it is.

"A lady of 90 who saw a tiny early photo of herself (aged 3) enlarged to A4 size suddenly saw the floor tiles of her grandparents' house and many memories came back. She recalled the layout of that room and the garden, the name of the dog and how she spent time at her grandparents' house." (London)

- If group leaders, carers and volunteers also bring photos everyone in the group will be represented. This can help to build up a sense of equality in the group, and also provide an opportunity for further story-telling between different people within the group.

"One person with dementia who always referred to the group leader as "Madame", changed this to "saluts poulette", (hello little chick), a term of endearment, once he had seen the photo of the group leader as a little girl. It enabled him to feel closer and more equal."

Brussels

- Another way of extending the use of the photos is to add captions and to build on these as more information is gathered. It may also be possible to link photos together if it turns out that two people lived near one another or had family in common.

'FAMILY MEMBERS'
DRAWING/A FAMILY TREE

Who was the most important person for you in your family?

- Talk in pairs or small groups about who was important and why. This may or may not be a parent. For some people, it might be a brother or sister and for others a grandparent with whom they had a particularly close relationship.

- Try to make a drawing or painting of the person concerned. A helper can do the drawing for the person with dementia asking for details of dress, hair and shoes, to put in the picture, and making suggestions, if they are not able to do it for themselves.

- Remember that in this activity it is **the process of making the picture and talking about it which is important**, not its artistic quality as an exhibition item.

  The resulting picture and the information it contains can be shared with the larger group and may evoke further memories for other group members.

- After the session, the picture may be taken home and used by a family carer to remind the person with dementia about what happened in the session and about the family member remembered.

"When we asked participants for pictures of their grandparents, one woman with dementia brought a wonderful photograph of her grandfather who had been working on a farm. On the photograph he held a strangely formed scythe and the group wondered what it was for.

Another man with dementia knew immediately that it was specially devised to harvest oats and he explained exactly how to use it. The woman, whose picture got so much attention was very pleased and kept asking her husband what her grandfather's name had been, assuming it was Johannes, the same as her husband's."

Kassel

- Gradually drawing up a family tree over a series of sessions can be another way of holding on to information emerging from the group or from other sources. It is helpful for volunteers and carers to have a sense of the family background of members of the group and to refer to family members in sessions so that the members feel "known".

'MY CHILDHOOD HOME'
A GUIDED TOUR AND A GROUND PLAN

This is a good topic for reminiscence and some people have very good visual and spatial recall where words present more problems.

"I said to my group of relatives and people with dementia from our residential home:
"Imagine that there is a map of Europe on the floor. Here is the north, the south, the east and west. If Paris is here, Lwow will be here, Budapest here, and so on... Please go and stand in the place where you were born." The carers helped their parents to find the right place. Lola's son, whose mother has Alzheimers, went to the wrong place. He had forgotten that he was not born in Paris and his mother reminded him that he was born during the war in a village in the south of France. We had much fun during this session."

Group leader, Paris

- One way of exploring this is to try going on an imaginary visit to the childhood home of the person with dementia.

- This can be done physically by a volunteer, carer or worker standing with the person with dementia, pretending to open the front door, moving from room to room, together reconstructing what was where.

  This must not feel like a test, but rather like an adventure in time, going back to explore a familiar place with tables, chairs, fireplaces, beds and pictures, all with their associations and in their special places

- Another way of doing the same exercise is to draw out the family home as a ground plan, or possibly just to concentrate on one important room. Some people who can say very little are able to produce quite detailed drawings of their own remembered childhood homes, showing the street and other local features when prompted by an interested listener who seeks more detail and offers helpful prompts.

- A variant on this approach is for the carer or volunteer to try to draw elements of what the person with dementia remembers, augmented by their own knowledge of the family home.

"My father's family is huge, and once I found a lot of photographs in the attic. I showed him the pictures and, to my surprise, he told me the names of his relatives and their relationship to him. He also told me stories about them."

Carer, Vienna

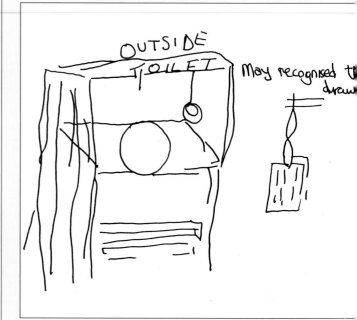

May (97) and her daughter Pat remember and draw the outside toilet during our childhood days session. (London)

Other people's memories, shared in the group, can provide considerable enjoyment for people with dementia who are not in a position to tell their own memory. It is important to look out for signs of enjoyment and identification and create opportunities for non-verbal participation.

'TOYS AND GAMES'
HANDLING AND PAINTING/DRAWING

Many people will remember toys they had or those they saw in shop windows which were unobtainable.

- Birthday and Christmas presents are often remembered including those which were a disappointment.

- The handling of old dolls, toy cars, teddies, building bricks and meccano will give pleasure and bring back memories. In small groups talk about a favourite toy, and then draw or paint it, with help if needed.

> *After her husband prompted her, a woman with dementia recalled her doll. Her father had returned to their bombed out house and rescued her favourite doll and the little china cups she liked to play with. She always loved her father for doing this and she still has the doll beside her bed. She became very animated when she remembered this. She recognised that at one level it was absurd to rescue these things which had no commercial value, as everyone else was rescuing valuables, but she also felt that it proved how much he loved her to rescue these things which were so important to her. All her emotions were re-awakened in telling this story. She said, "Just to think he went back in to get my doll."*

Kassel

'MEALTIMES'
A TABLEAU COMES TO LIFE

People may remember the rituals associated with family meals in childhood, such as prayers before and after eating, waiting for Father to arrive, only certain people being allowed to speak, mother never sitting down, the best food being given to Father and the boys, and everyone having their own place at the table.

- If someone in the group has strong memories, ask them to pose the rest of the group as though they were members of their family.

- Take an imaginary or real photograph of this tableau and then ask the 'author' to help the group to bring it to life, by giving 'mother', 'father' and others typical things to say and do.

'FAVOURITE CHILDHOOD RECIPES'
PUTTING MEMORIES IN THE BOWL

This topic might include favourite recipes prepared by mothers and grandmothers.

- A useful way into these memories is to pass around a plate or bowl and ask members of the group to hold the bowl and call to mind a favourite or most hated dish from childhood.

- Some people will remember how the dish was made and the circumstances in which it was prepared and eaten.

- Others may just say "jelly" or "stew" and whatever people offer should be accepted. It is not meant to be a memory test, but an opportunity for sharing spontaneous pleasure and humour.

Family carers may remember a speciality of their person's mother and share this first with their person and then with the group in a spontaneous way, eg *"I was just thinking of Mary's mother who made the most delicious plum cake, didn't she?"*, thus bringing in the person with dementia and including their life in the pool of stories of the group, even though the person with dementia is no longer able to articulate the story for themselves. It is however, worth waiting to see what people with dementia offer spontaneously in these 'round the group' sessions as they are often able to participate more fully than carers expect and it would be unhelpful to pre-empt their independent participation.

'FAVOURITE CHILDHOOD FOODS'
COOKING AND MAKING A RECIPE BOOK

- An extension of this exercise is to actually cook some of the favourite remembered recipes if workers or other volunteers are willing to co-operate or if the family carers are willing to make an experiment at home.

In the Norwegian group, there was an enjoyable pancake making session, with all the pleasure of eating the food together afterwards and sharing memories of pancake days in the past. They did however find that it was very important to give the people with dementia tasks where they could succeed, as failure led to negative feelings when one lady who dropped an egg was so embarrassed that she left the group. (Oslo)

- It is important to find ways of involving people with dementia in familiar practical tasks (domestic or otherwise) where they can make a positive contribution and feel valued in the group. In the day centre for people with dementia to which the RYCT Stockholm project was attached, it is a matter of course for the people with dementia to help in preparing lunch and to eat it all together with staff, volunteers and carers. The sense of normality and belonging increases the morale of all concerned.

- A recipe book of favourite recipes from childhood may be too ambitious for some groups, but this subject is very absorbing and recording the recipes and something about the mothers who made them can be a manageable way to produce a small booklet which can be shared outside the group and can draw attention to what it is still possible for people with dementia to remember and do.

'HOUSEHOLD CHORES'
PRACTISING REMEMBERED SKILLS

These are a good source of reminiscences and apply to men and women equally. Both can often remember running errands, collecting firewood, cutting up newspaper for toilet paper, polishing silver, cleaning out the hens, turning the mangle handle and helping to hang out the washing.

- Useful props would be:
  - ✔ firewood or kindling
  - ✔ newspaper and scissors
  - ✔ a small mangle or a rubbing board
  - ✔ old-fashioned wooden clothes pegs.

- Often father had particular tasks in the home, such as mending the boots and shoes, or (less happily) disciplining the children. Trying to remember them in action helps to bring family figures alive again. Doing some of the remembered activities again (not the disciplining!) is pleasurable for all, and as the body remembers the actions, so the related memories of people and places can come back too.

- The introduction of smells associated with actions or activities can also act as powerful triggers, for example using silver polish, or the smell of damp washing and hard soap.

"In Norway, group members sharpened knives with sand and soap as they used to do when they were young - an unpleasant chore from the past, but one which voked lots of memories."
Oslo

'PUNISHMENTS'
ACTING OUT

There are often many stories about being naughty when young and what happened when you were caught out.

- After sharing memories of childhood pranks and misdemeanours in small group try acting one of the stories and show it to the rest of the group. Allow time for the rest of the group to say what memories are sparked off for them by the enactment.

- Alternatively you could talk about who was responsible for discipline in your home when you were young and what punishments were given.

'WASHDAY'
PRACTISING REMEMBERED SKILLS

This topic usually brings back strong memories for many people, including memories of the hard work involved in washing and drying clothes without modern machines.

- A mangle or washboard and the opportunity to show how washing used to be done may be enjoyed even by people who have difficulty articulating memories.

- Using real water and soap and really wet cotton or wool and feeling the weight of wet washing in their hands can act as a powerful trigger.

'ILLNESS AND HOME REMEDIES'
SENSORY STIMULATION

This is another rich topic, although for some who may have lost members of their family to illness, it may also be a sad one. Some people may have been in hospital with scarlet fever or other infectious diseases and photographs of local hospitals in the past may stimulate discussion.

- There were many medicines used by mothers and a little research by leaders can produce names which can help trigger memories.

- Some of the home remedies, for example eucalyptus, are still obtainable, and may be passed around for people to smell.

- Participants may remember how their mother or granny used to persuade them to take a dose of nasty-tasting medicine for example *"down the little red lane'* and then a *'sweetie'* to follow.

'BATHTIME'
DISCUSSION AND ACTING OUT

This includes remembering having a bath in front of the fire, filling and emptying the bath and sharing the water with brothers and sisters.

● An old cast iron tub of any description is a powerful reminder and if anyone in the group is willing to sit in the tub and pretend to be "bathed" by another member as "mother" the result can be hilarious.

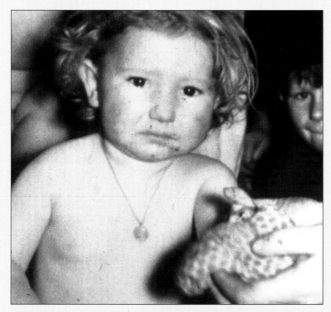

Bath time remembered. This photo of a child being washed in a tin bath is taken from the Recall pack produced by Help The Aged in London.

'BEDTIME'
DISCUSSION AND HANDLING

Bed time rituals and memories can be shared, including having a candle to light your way to bed, night time prayers, sharing a bed with brothers and sisters, babies sleeping in a drawer or cupboard, songs sung by parents and older siblings to get little ones to sleep.

● Use props such as stone hot-water bottles as memory triggers and encourage members of the group to handle the items.

● Some members of the group may be happy to join in the flow of others' memories by listening and nodding while looking at and handling old objects.

> **"A woman with dementia remembered that as a child when her parents went out at night her brother used to get her out of bed to play with his train set. One night, her father came back and he pretended not to see them playing as he did not want to spoil their fun."**
> **Kassel**

Members of the group enjoy playing remembered childhood games. (Brussels)

CLOSING ACTIVITY

● Ask the group to remember favourite songs their mother or granny sang them including bed time songs. Sing them in the group.

● Are there some special phrases people remember which their mothers used to say to them at bedtime, like "Goodnight, sleep tight" or "Up the wooden hill"?

● Perhaps there was a special prayer which people remember saying before going to sleep, like *"God bless Mummy and God bless Daddy and make me a very good girl. Amen".*

ACTIVITIES TO TRY OUTSIDE THE GROUP

● Try to contact someone who knew the person with dementia and other members of their family when they were young, either a relative or friend, and ask them to write down or record some of their memories from that time.

● If they live near, invite them to come round and share these memories. If they are able to come, spend some time before they arrive reminding the person with dementia who the visitor is.

● If there is a local museum of childhood in your area, try to organise a visit there.

● It is often possible to find replica scraps which may be cut out and put into a scrapbook, which is a pleasurable remembered activity from childhood.

● Label early photos on the back with names and places and have them available when people call in so that they can discuss them with the person with dementia.

● Prepare a family tree over a period of time, adding in members and photos where possible.

● Try cooking together some remembered favourite dish from childhood.

MY NEIGHBOURHOOD

This subject takes members out of their childhood home and into the neighbourhoods where they lived and played when they were young. Leaders need to be aware that participants may come from very different backgrounds. Some, for instance, may have been born in a rural area or even in another country. Triggers will need to take account of this and reflect a range of experience wherever possible. Topics could include street sellers, local shops, running errands, neighbours, friends, games, nearby parks or open ground, woods, canals and rivers.

TRIGGERS

skipping ropes, dice, stones, cigarette cards, conkers, marbles, hoops, spinning tops, diabolo, chalk, a leather football, a simple home-made kite, chestnuts, recorded sounds, horse-shoes, grasses or straw.

STARTERS

- Ask the group to call out the cries they remember, such as "Rag Bone", "coalman, coal", the muffin man and his bell, the cat's meat man, etc. Try to make a sound collage from all these sounds. You can add in horse's hooves, passing trains, ships' hooters, bird song, sea-gulls, tram bells, or anything else which comes to mind.

- Making a sound as a group is fun, and the group leader can ensure that it doesn't just feel like a noise by agreeing a signal for starting and finishing it, making it louder and softer and even bringing out solos, etc.

> Bear in mind that the result of this sort of exercise will be different each time and that this does not matter. The unexpected must be a source of pleasure, not irritation.

Mothers, circa 1925, Copenhagen

- The group leader can mark out the chalk lines for playing hopscotch and invite members to explain how to do it. Some members may want to try playing themselves.

- A game of marbles played on the floor between members and helpers will remind people in the group of competitions with friends, favourite marbles won, lost or stolen and the complicated rules of the game.

ACTIVITIES
'MY STREET'
SHOWING ROUND AND DRAWING

- In pairs or small groups think about the view from the front door of the childhood home. This exercise could be done in discussion or actually performed by opening the imaginary front door and walking into the street or countryside. Memories could be triggered about neighbours, friends, local shops.

> *A carer who happened to have grown up in the same part of town as a man with dementia started to recall all kinds of activities that they used to do as children. For instance in winter they were tobogganing down a big street right into the entrance gates of the houses. The man with dementia enjoyed these stories very much and gave his comments, like: "We were lucky when there was no tram coming at the moment we crossed the street on our sleighs". When the carer recalled the names of some of the boys living in the street at the time, the man with dementia said: "Oh, he was a real tough one," and "I didn't mix with them because they went to another school". The wife of this man was very moved and felt that she could never have helped her husband with these memories as she did not know anything about the street life at that time.*
>
> Kassel

- Walking, remembering and showing is an enjoyable activity for many people with dementia, and they will like listening to others' descriptions, doubtless remembering much of their own experience without necessarily being able to recall it verbally. Look out for signs of pleasurable recognition on these 'guided tours', such as nodding, smiling, looking interested or amused. This showing round activity leads very naturally into making a ground plan of the street, showing neighbours, local shops, passing traders, horse-drawn vehicles, local characters, children skipping in the street, a nearby park.

Boys outside their childhood home in 1920s. (London)

'RUNNING ERRANDS'
DISCUSSION AND ACTING OUT

Many group members will have run errands when they were young, perhaps running to the corner shop (for city dwellers) where things were bought fresh every day in the small quantities which were affordable.

> *"Many of the participants remembered being sent to get milk in an open can with a handle. They had all tried to swing round the can full of milk so fast that none of it spilled. When the group leader asked him, a man with dementia got up and demonstrated with a milk can how you had to swing it around so that no drop was spilled."*
>
> **Kassel**

- Useful prompts for this are blue paper bags, butter pats, co-op coupons or books, ration books, a purse with old money, a cup for putting a spoonful of jam in, a shopping basket, a small barrow, a pawn shop token

- Many older people remember their parents (or themselves) having to ask for goods on tick (on credit) and might enjoy playing out the roles of reluctant shop-keeper and wheedling mum or heart-melting child.

- Other popular acting out subjects are wartime queueing, where people joined a line without knowing what they were queueing for. All sorts of things went on in these queues as people got into conversation with others, and bargained for rationed goods.

- People with dementia often react favourably and spontaneously to such opportunities to act out, especially if the prevailing atmosphere is one of high good humour, where everyone is willing to take risks and lose a bit of dignity in the interests of fun.

'CHILDHOOD FRIENDSHIPS'
DRAWING AND PAINTING

- These were often very strong. There may be memories of best friends, what you did together, what happened when you quarrelled and how you made up.

- After talking about friends in pairs or a small group draw a picture of your best friends, or help some one else draw or paint a picture of theirs.

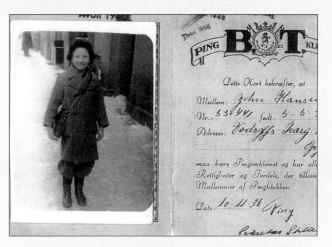

A club card from a member of our group reminded many others of children's clubs they had belonged to when young. (Copenhagen)

'STREET GAMES'
DISCUSSION AND HANDLING

This is an enjoyable topic to explore in practical ways as well as through conversation.

- Playing the games and, if possible, handling the objects associated with them is the most lively way to remember what games were played in younger days and all the associated rules, and of course the friends one played them with.

- People from different parts of the country often have different names for games and variations in the way they were played, but there is plenty of overlap and it is fun to compare.

● Remembering where the games were played might bring in a discussion of local parks, stretches of countryside, local woodlands, the street or a stretch of waste ground or a special 'den' or secret meeting place.

Playing in the street: a good reminiscence topic for our group (London)

● There is a section in the schooldays topic on childhood games which were played in the playground and on the way to school and you may wish to link with this.

'SONGS AND RHYMES'
SINGING, RECITATION AND ACTIONS

"We were looking at childhood toys in our group and someone showed us a spinning top. Suddenly my wife began singing a song about tops which I had never heard her sing. She remembered it as she held the top in her hands. She could then remember some other things she did as a child. I thought, "How is this possible?" Something returned to her and it was good for both of us, as we had a bit of contact through this."

Carer, Amsterdam

● Songs and rhymes connected with childhood games are often remembered and the singing or recitation of them helps people to remember the actions. Often if the group leader does not know

the actions this is an advantage, the group can teach her or him and the game can be played out by several group members.

● **Ring songs like "The farmer's in the den" or "Brown girl in the ring" can be sung by the whole group with the most physically able playing the different parts. Skipping songs too are often remembered and remind the group members of how skilled they were. They may well be a means of remembering friends (and enemies) from the street or neighbourhood who joined in these games or bad-tempered neighbours who tried to put a stop to them.**

● **Remembering games which were specially designed to upset neighbours are a good source of humour, such as "Knocking down Ginger" in England or the Dutch tradition of "Lazy Day" which involved children making a huge noise with dustbin lids on one night of the year and waking all the adults up very early in the morning.**

CLOSING ACTIVITY

● It is a good idea to close this neighbourhood topic with a song which reinforces local belonging, while being careful to include people who are not from the locality.

ACTIVITIES TO TRY OUTSIDE THE GROUP

● If it is possible to make a visit back to the childhood street, even if it has changed a lot, this can be a very powerful experience. Being on the same ground, seeing where the school, shops and park were in relation to the home street; these are effective memory triggers. It can be a highly charged emotional event to revisit a place of one's youth, but this can be a very positive way of making connections with one's younger self.

● It is important to bring the person back to the present, encouraging them to see the advantages as well as disadvantages of their current home. Local history museums and libraries may well be able to loan photos of the area as it was and these can be useful triggers for remembering at home.

● Making a collage of photos and memories connected with a local area could be an enjoyable ongoing activity for the person with dementia and their carer. It can also act as a stimulus for conversation or practical contributions (such as photos, objects or memories) from visiting relatives or friends who may have connections with the area.

SCHOOLDAYS

People with dementia often have strong memories of the years they spent at school. Topics which might bring back memories include the first day at school, the journey to school, favourite or worst teachers, dinner-times and going home for lunch, games played in the playground, bullying, corporal punishments, best friends and leaving school. Remember that some people may not have been to school for very long, or even at all. The war years interrupted many people's education, some people missed school because their labour was needed to supplement the family income and others were taught privately by tutors, by governesses at home or even by their own parents. These people need to be included in the group and their experience reflected.

TRIGGERS

Slates, chalk, satchel or school bag, inkpot, dipping pen, ruler, skipping rope, marbles, paper dart, school report, example of handwriting, a whistle, items of school clothing such as ties, caps or gym knickers.

Schooldays remembered (Kassel)

A 1922 school report, bringing back memories of loved and hated teachers (London)

STARTERS

● The session might begin with a well-known song or hymn from schooldays, for example, *'All Things Bright and Beautiful'*. Singing is a powerful way of bringing the group together and also very often began the school day, together with prayers, in assembly.

● Invite the group to imagine they are in a classroom in the 1920's or 1930's or the classroom when they were at school, and to tell the leader and the rest of the group what might be on the walls, and in the room, for example, maps, diagrams, pictures of the Royal family, desks, canes, times-tables. At this point do not encourage long narratives, but use this as an exercise to take the group back to a shared past.

● It is not always necessary to go round the group systematically as some members may not be able to contribute and others may feel they are being tested. Just let people pitch in as they feel like it.

● Pass round a schoolbag and ask members of the group to say one thing they might have had in their schoolbag - for example, an apple or homework. Again this can be a one-word activity, and not all those in the group may want to participate, so be ready as leader to contribute suggestions and maintain momentum.

ACTIVITIES

'THE JOURNEY TO SCHOOL' DISCUSSION

● Talk about how members of the group got to school, whether they walked, if school was near home or a long way away.

● Town and country journeys could be compared, and a record made of different ways individuals got to school.

● Find out who went home for dinners and the sort of meals their mothers prepared for them. It might be possible to obtain information about this from the carer or relatives before the meeting so that those who have trouble recalling names and details can be helped to retrieve their memories successfully.

Fritz Adensamer's first school day, September, 1915 (Vienna)

'OBJECTS FROM THE CLASSROOM' HANDLING AND DISCUSSION

● Lay out objects connected with schooldays, such as a pencil box, a map, a satchel, and ask members of the group to select one. Make sure all members can easily choose an object, perhaps with help of volunteers or, working as a whole group, pass round a single tray of objects or an old schoolbag containing the objects, and allow each member to choose one which interests them.

● Then discuss the chosen object in a small group or with one other person. You may have a group where each person is happy to tell the whole group about the associations or memories of objects.

● In pairs, approach the collection of objects, choose one and take it back to join a small group to use as a trigger to start talking about school days. Where members can no longer easily recall or articulate memories, objects themselves may be enjoyed with a volunteer or carer.

> **"Nellie and a volunteer handled a slate with shells, feeling the objects and playing with them. At one point the volunteer suggested the shells might be sheep. The absurdity of this amused Nellie who laughed as the volunteer 'herded' the shells into a corner. "**
>
> **Bradford, U.K**

● A leader or helper might hold up different objects and invite response from any member of the group, perhaps identifying the object, or showing how it was used, or telling a story connected with the object. While some members may not speak out, they may nevertheless enjoy hearing others' stories which may then trigger memories of their own.

'POEMS AND MULTIPLICATION TABLES' RECITATION

● Whole group recitation is a good way of taking members back to their schooldays. Things learned in childhood are often well preserved and even those who appear to have little ability to recall, may join in with a poem, times-tables or weights and measures, learned 'by rote' when young.

> **"A carer told us that one day at home she had begun to recite a long poem by Goethe. When she stopped, her husband recited the rest of the poem to the end."**
>
> **Vienna**

'BACK IN THE CLASSROOM'
WRITING

● Bring some dipping pens or old-fashioned fountain pens, blotting paper, and prepare some paper with lines on as handwriting guides. Some members may enjoy having a go, while others may enjoy watching the leader attempting to write something on the blackboard. It is important to find ways of including all group members when planning activities.

"When the group leader gave a text written in Gothic lettering to one of the participants who suffered from dementia, he eagerly took it and read the whole text out with his lovely strong voice. He felt very proud when the younger group members assured him that they had never learned how to write and read gothic and were glad he had helped them to understand what was written on the sheet. Everybody in the group then remembered if they had ever learned this writing and the trouble some of them had experienced when trying to read their parents' and grandparents' writing."

Kassel

An example of Gothic handwriting, which triggered many memories in our group. (Kassel)

'WHEN I WAS AT SCHOOL'
DRAWING

● In pairs or small groups, share memories of schooldays, and then draw a picture of the person with dementia at school, either in the classroom or outside in the playground, holding something, or with a friend. This could be done jointly with a volunteer or carer, or by a helper or carer of themselves if the person with dementia has difficulty remembering. If the person with dementia has difficulty communicating, then watch for a positive response, such as a smile or a change in facial expression, as the drawing is made. This type of exercise is not about producing works of art, but about using the process of drawing to evoke and elicit memories and then recording these memories on paper.

"One couple knew each other from their school days and the wife, who suffered from dementia loved to tell the group, how much she had enjoyed going to school and how well she got along with her classmates. By and by she felt towards the other participants as if they were her classmates and she kept saying: "We all get along so well with each other, we are in the same school, you know.""

Kassel

'TALKING IN CLASS'
ACTING OUT

● Pick a school event and try acting as if the situation was happening now. This can be done with the whole group or by dividing into small groups and preparing something to show to the whole group.

Acting out is fun. It can promote a group feeling, give new life and a new dimension to a perhaps often-told story and give a real buzz to those who 'have a go'. If the risk is minimised by the group leader, the rewards for those who participate are great. Seeing other people's stories acted out can stimulate a lot of additional memories and associations as familiar situations are recognised. The creativity and humour generated by bringing memories to life in this way, lifts the energy and atmosphere of the group.

● The group leader can ask for examples of classroom misdemeanours and punishments, for instance being late, not doing homework, talking in class, flicking paper pellets, making a spelling mistake, not knowing the answer.

● Then take one story and act it out. For example, if someone says they got into trouble for being late, try performing the scene spontaneously by pretending to be the teacher and asking the rest of the group to suggest what the teacher might say, and suggest excuses given by the pupil.

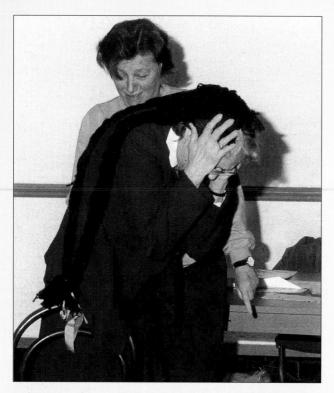

Joan remembered being a naughty girl and tying her friend's plaits to the back of her chair. When her friend tried to get up to answer the teacher's question, she could not do so as the heavy wooden chair was attached. Joan got into trouble. The group acted out this story with everyone being the children in the classroom and one of the group leaders being the teacher. This brought back a lot of other memories of classroom mischief which were very entertaining for the whole group. (London)

- In small groups of three or four share stories of school punishments, and plan how to show one of the stories to the rest of the group either by a brief enactment or by the narration of a story by a volunteer or carer. There may be members of the group who lack the ability or confidence to 'go front of stage' but who nevertheless by being part of the group, can share in the recognition and rewards of a performance and applause.

'THE PLAYGROUND'
HANDLING AND DISCUSSION

This is a rich source of memories for many people. Chalk for hopscotch, skipping ropes and marbles can be brought in to help trigger memories of rhymes and games played in the playground.

- Examples brought to the meeting by the group leader can act as prompts, for instance 'Oranges and Lemons', and 'The farmer's in his den' (see childhood section for further examples).

- Other playground topics might include the different things boys and girls did in the playground, learning how to hop, whistle, skip,

losing front teeth etc. Talking about gangs and bullies will probably stimulate memories of rivalries and dares, which might be recorded and shared or acted out in a larger group.

> **❝The daughter of someone with dementia began to talk about when she was summoned to the head teacher for having rubbed snow in the face of a boy she was fond of. Her mother's spontaneous and 'accusatory' comment was: "You never told me that before!" This subsequently provoked a lot of laughter in the group and the incident showed that people can still get to know new things about each other many years after such events. It was also a situation in which the daughter felt that her mother (with dementia) was acting as a mother and this was positive for the daughter.❞**

Stockholm

'FAVOURITE AND LEAST FAVOURITE TEACHERS'
WRITING

- Stories and descriptions of teachers and the subjects they taught could be gathered and recorded. An imaginary school report could be made using group members' memories.

- Local libraries or museums (or individual group members) may have examples of real reports or school log books which could act as triggers. Some people may even have kept their school reports or head teacher's testimonials.

A Danish school class photo from 1948 brought to our schooldays session (Copenhagen)

'MISSING SCHOOL'
STORY TELLING AND ACTING OUT

Young people often missed long periods of school for a number of reasons, such as childhood illnesses, looking after brothers and sisters, helping in the home or with parents' market stalls, helping at harvest time or keeping the crows off the crops. Others played truant and were caught by the truancy officer and taken back to their parents for 'sorting out'.

- Exchange stories about scrapes people got into and try acting out some of these experiences

'SCHOOL PHOTOGRAPHS'
GROUP PHOTOGRAPHS

- Some members may have school photographs which could be shown to the group. A school group photograph could also be taken with participants imagining they are back at school. Memories could be shared of what they wore, and who best friends were, making a silly face when the photo was taken, etc. The resulting photograph could be enjoyed by the group the following week.

People in our group had kept their old school photos and we enjoyed handing them round. (Kassel)

'SPECIAL SCHOOL DAYS'
TABLEAU

- Special days such as Empire Day, harvest festivals, prize giving, sports days are often vividly remembered. Local libraries may have photographs of school related events and activities, or members of the group may themselves have photographs they could share with the group.

- After discussion pose the group as though they are involved in one of these activities. Take an imaginary (or real photo) and then maybe ask the group to bring the photo to life for ten seconds, moving slightly and saying or singing one phrase.

CLOSING ACTIVITIES

- After discussion about how the school day ended choose a hymn or school song which is familiar and sing it together as a group. Ask group members to say in one word or one sentence how they felt on their last day at school, making sure that only those who have the confidence and wish to, take part.

ACTIVITIES TO TRY OUTSIDE THE GROUP

- Carers or relatives could take the person they are caring for back to their school, and even go inside and have a look around. If the building is still in use, comparisons could be made between how it used to be and how it is today. A photograph could be taken and brought to show to the group the following week.

> **When we were standing outside her school, Mother became very glad and lively, pointed out where her classroom, the gymnastics, the swimming pool, etc, were. She talked quite a while about swimming at school and talked about when she had started the public middle school at Sofia. She also remembered that she didn't want to go on studying there later, but wanted to become a hairdresser instead. During the week, I looked for and gave to my mother a couple of her old school books, which triggered many memories. We both had a very pleasant time when we talked about this and other things.**
>
> **Stockholm**

- Grandchildren might talk to the carer and the person with dementia about their experiences of school and compare these with memories of how school used to be. They might look at different ways of handwriting, for instance, or school reports. The latest skipping rhymes could be recited, and skipping techniques demonstrated.

- If the person with dementia has lots of positive memories from their schooldays, songs, games, jokes and catch phrases from school could become part of the carer's repertoire. These could be enjoyed through the day with the person with dementia telling their own stories when a memory is triggered.

- Siblings or friends of the person with dementia could be approached for memories and stories about the person with dementia when they were in school.

THE WORLD OF WORK

Sharing memories of working lives is often a good way to make connections between people in a reminiscence group. People may discover that they worked for the same employer or had a similar apprenticeship or trades in common.

Topics to explore under this theme include first jobs, the journey to work, the working day, uniforms, break-times, machinery, difficult or kind bosses, accidents at work, pay disputes, workplace friendships, moving to another town to look for work. This is a good theme for men in the group who sometimes feel unsure how to contribute on more personal subjects.

TRIGGERS

Tools, ruler, measuring tape, type-writer, wage packet, 'ready reckoner', apprenticeship certificates, photographs of different work-places, tapes of machinery noise, office stationery, washing boards, irons, duster, maid's apron, photos of local factories

STARTERS

● Lay out a selection of work related items, and invite people to choose one which interests them. Include items connected with housework and domestic service so that women are not excluded.

● Pass each object around in turn, talk about what it was used for and how it worked.

● Begin with leaders and other volunteers miming their first jobs, then see if anyone else wants to have a go. Everyone else has to guess what that job is. The people with dementia may need some help to decide on an action which can represent their work, but will probably enjoy having the opportunity to take part in the game. Otherwise a helper can take responsibility for showing their job to the rest of the group, or they can do it together. Some jobs are hard to act, but the activity leads to much amusement and people with dementia are often very good at guessing.

Leslie looks at an old wooden with Maggie. He goes on to draw the plane for his own satisfaction. Drawing is sometimes less of a struggle than talking. (London)

Ove Dahl, Danish group leader, stirs memories with a glazier's tool bag. (Copenhagen)

> **"A man whose dementia was very much advanced so that he never spoke, was very pleased to hold a wooden inch scale, folded and stretched it for quite a long time, smiling and perhaps remembering working as a joiner."**
> **Kassel**

- Ask carers to gather objects, pictures or documents to do with working life which might trigger memories for the person they care for. Bring these in a suitable bag (for example a brief case or a tool bag) to the session on work.

> **"One participant often thinks that he is still at work. He loved his work and treated it as his hobby and is upset to think that he cannot go there any more. So his wife often invents excuses for him not to go to work that day and makes pretend phone calls to his office. This may sound a little strange, but it satisfies her husband. This carer prepared a special bag of objects and she brought this to the session,. She placed the bag on his lap and asked him to talk about what was in it. It appeared to him to be his old office-case with all the well-known contents in it like a luncheon box, an apple, an (old) diary, a pen and notebook. He began to tell how he went to the office, sometimes by bicycle, most of the time walking, practising for 'The Vierdaagse' (a famous yearly walking-event that lasts four days). He found a medal of the Dutch Walking Association in his luncheon-box. He told that his work had always been his hobby and that he even reached the Guinness Book of Records because of working for 72 years with the same boss. The other carers asked him a lot of questions and at the end, he told that he had stopped working two years ago, which was remarkable because at home he had never before acknowledged this."**
> **Amsterdam**

ACTIVITIES

'CHILDHOOD AMBITIONS'
REMEMBERED DREAMS AND FANTASIES

- Remember when you were young and share with others in a small group what your dreams and ambitions were 'When I grow up I want to be a ...' These can be fantasy ambitions, for example, 'cowboy' or 'film star' or more realistic ambitions such as an engineer or a teacher. Encourage people to say what was attractive about this fantasy and how they imagined themselves in the part.

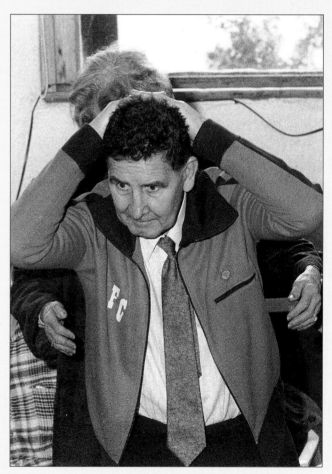

Jim mimes his job as a P.E. instructor. (London)

'LEAVING SCHOOL'
DISCUSSION AND HANDLING

- Go into small groups and talk about leaving school. What was their first job and how did they get it? If the leader can find out beforehand where participants worked, appropriate triggers may be brought to the session, for example photographs of a similar work-place, equipment or tools. It is often fascinating to hear about the long apprenticeships people served in the past, how seriously they took their trade and what their relations with their boss were like. People may have held on to certificates and official scrolls connected with their qualification.

First job as a sales assistant, 1924 (Kassel)

'MY FIRST PAY PACKET'
LISTING

● Ask members what was in their first pay packet and what they spent it on. Many people gave their wages to their parents when they were young, and were just given a bit of pocket money for themselves. It might be interesting to list all the things people did with their first pay, like buying stockings, lipstick or cigarettes. Try this, making separate columns for men and women.

Edith remembered how to unlock the keyboard of this old typewriter when all the younger members of the group failed. She greatly enjoyed putting paper through the rollers and feeling the keys beneath her fingers. (London)

'REMEMBERING OLD SKILLS'
ACTION

● Memory of physical actions often remains strong. Old actions from work or home such as typewriting, sewing machine work, and the handling of familiar work tools can give a lot of pleasure to people whose verbal memory may be quite poor.

● However not everyone retains these abilities, and so it is important to offer them in ways which avoid testing. Some may enjoy looking at and handling a tool they used to be competent to use, while others may want to 'have a go'.

"Mary worked in the spinning shed of a local textile mill. Photographs of textile machinery and a tin containing machinery parts and tools were brought to the work topic meeting. Mary found the smell of the tools very evocative, and was able to explain in detail how the machines in the photographs worked.".

Bradford

Winifred holding a photo of herself and fellow workers in the 'plain and decorated tin factory where she worked when she was young. (Bradford)

'LOOKING THE PART'
DRESSING UP

● Borrow uniforms from a museum and invite helpers or people with dementia to try them on and 'be' a bus conductor or a nurse. Take a real or imaginary photograph of the group or of individuals, and maybe ask people in the photo to say one word or sentence about what they are doing or feeling or remembering.

'THE WORKING DAY'
MAKING CHARTS AND TIME-TABLES

● Talk in small groups about the hours of work people remember and their rates of pay at the start of their working lives. People often remember these details and it is worth writing them down as a list or chart and seeing who had the longest day. Shop work and domestic service will be strong candidates.

● Think also about how far people travelled to work and how they got there, comparing 'then' with 'now'. It is quite an interesting task to try to draw up a remembered timetable with people in the group, from the time they got up in the morning right through to bed time, showing how long people were at their work place and what they did on a typical evening.

'A WOMAN'S WORK'
USING OBJECTS, SHARING SKILLS

● For many women 'work' in the past meant housework. Talk about the work that went into keeping a household and looking after the family - the physical work, the pride in having everything nice, spring cleaning, and how different it is for people today.

● Other possible topics include budgeting on uncertain incomes and the impact of family allowances and pensions. Use objects connected with housework so that members of the group can remember past skills through physical actions. It might be interesting to bring some young women in to meet the group to compare notes on how domestic work is done today.

> DRESSMAKING, Costumes, Renovating; at lady's own house.—Write, 127, Courthill-road, Lewisham. 25
> DRESSMAKING; good style, fit; moderate charges.—Boore, 119, Mount Pleasant-road, Lewisham. 8
> MISS MILLARD, Dressmaker, Costumier.— Customers' Material made up; moderate charges.—64, Murillo-rd, Lewisham. 8
> CUTTER and Fitter, able to take complete charge 16 girls; first class work only; also Apprentices and Assistants; Lewisham. —Write, Box 432, "Kentish Mercury," S.E.10. 25
> SIX Apprentices for best West End work; also Assistants and Hands, St. John's district.—Write, Box 431, "Kentish Mercury," S.E.10. 25

Situations Vacant advertisement, local newspaper, 1930s (London)

● For some a session on work provides an opportunity to show the skills and capabilities they have had in the past and allows the carer and other members of the group to appreciate the whole person and their achievements.

> **"A woman who had not been very well settled found a place in the group after a session where she showed pieces of writing she had done when she was younger. Although she was not able to speak very much the pieces of writing were enjoyed by other group members who then felt they 'knew' the woman better, and appreciated what she had achieved."**
> **Brussels**

Many women undertook challenging new work roles during the war years, often moving a long way from home for the first time and learning skills they would never have dreamed of in peace time. For some women, these years provide exhilarating memories and they enjoy talking about the camaraderie which many of them recall from that period. It is important to allow time for people to consider the changes they have lived through in their working lives, without fearing too much the potential dangers surrounding 'the war years' as a reminiscence topic.

However for some people with dementia the memory of what they achieved in the past has gone and they find it puzzling to be confronted with something they do not recognise. Some people do not enjoy being reminded of skills they no longer possess and may be frustrated or upset by what they produced in the past.

● Ask if anyone has kept apprenticeship certificates, awards for excellence, badges, 'congratulations on your retirement' letters and pass them round the group. If carers or relatives have access to such items, ask them to send them or bring them along to the group. It is a good opportunity to recognise and congratulate people all over again for what they have achieved.

ACTIVITIES TO TRY OUTSIDE THE GROUP

● Take the person with dementia back to where they used to work. Where possible, go inside to see if anything is still the same. Get in touch with some one who used to work with them and see if they can come along too and share memories with the person with dementia. Take photographs and bring them back to the group the following week.

> **"After our session on starting work, when I got home I asked my friend to tell me about her days as a district nurse and it was incredible what she could remember. Yet she forgets what has been said to her five minutes ago."**
> **Carer, London**

● Think about ways in which the person with dementia can do things which help regain the feeling of being useful which they had when they were working

> **"Vera's daughter ran a garden centre business. Every day she would take her mother with her for some of the time and find little things for her to do in the shop. This gave her mother pleasure and the feeling of being useful, and reminded her daughter that some of her mother's social and business skills were still there."**
> **Kassel**

DRESSING UP, LOOKING GOOD AND GOING OUT

This subject will be especially enjoyable if you can borrow or find a range of objects and triggers which will remind people of their early adult lives. Topics include first shaves, the first kiss, using lipstick and powder for the first time, going out with friends and seeing a girl or boy you liked, going out to cinemas and dance halls, getting home late, and favourite outfits.

TRIGGERS

Fabrics, stockings, handkerchiefs, shaving equipment, cinema tickets, lipstick , costume jewellery, theatre programmes, big band dance records, an old gramophone, gloves, stiff collars, old magazines adverts for local dance halls, photos of film stars

STARTERS

● Ask group members to bring a photograph of themselves when 'dressed up and looking good' or an item of clothing or jewellery from when they were young adults. Pass these round the group and enjoy them together.

❝Two ladies with dementia had a wonderful time packing and unpacking a hand-bag and showing the flashy objects - lipstick, powder case, perfume - to each other.❞

Kassel

● Ask group members to bring in (or tell the group leader about) a favourite piece of music or song and play some of these at the beginning of the session, allowing time to listen to the memories triggered by hearing or singing them.

ACTIVITIES

'IN MY BAG'
DISCUSSION AND HANDLING

● Fill some small elegant bags from different periods with small objects connected with going out, for instance, make-up, jewellery, perfume ('Evening in Paris' was a popular brand in England), a cigarette case, a dance card, a tram ticket. In small groups enjoy these objects and talk about the memories evoked by them.

● For men, fill an equivalent bag with a comb, a silk scarf, a stiff collar and shaving utensils. Let them feel the brush and the shaving cream. Talk about their first shave, electric shavers, shaves in barbers' shops and how they got ready to go out dancing or to the pictures.

❝The gentlemen demonstrated how one shaved with soap and a soft brush.❞

Oslo

A three-dimensional exhibition of a 1930s dance hall evokes happy and romantic memories (London)

May, Lil and Joyce have fun trying on hats and gloves from a 1930s collection. (London)

'FASHIONS OF THE TIME'
DRESSING UP

● Bring boxes of costume jewellery and old dresses. Try some of these on to show the fashions at different periods.

● Bring some photographs or magazines, and talk about dress and hair styles worn by members of the group when they were young. Don't forget to include men in this exercise as they might have been just as fashion conscious. Try on hats, gloves, scarves and shoes and pose for a group photograph

'A FAVOURITE OUTFIT'
DISCUSSION AND DRAWING

● Draw a picture (or describe and have someone else draw a picture), of a favourite outfit members had when they were young, remembering colours, textures and where the outfits were bought or made. What accessories did they have to go with their favourite outfit and where did they wear it?

● It might be possible to bring in a number of dolls, old and new, and look at their outfits and talk about changing fashions. Old paper patterns are interesting to open up and look at, and many people will remember dresses they made for themselves.

"Edith was looking at pictures of dresses in the 1930s. She said, "Yes, that was the style, pink was the colour. They had a frill on the bottom and no sleeves usually". She chose a pink pen and started to draw a dress. "Pink is a warm colour", she commented."

Volunteer observation, London

'THE SILVER SCREEN'
WATCHING FILMS AND TALKING ABOUT THEM

● Favourite films are a good source of reminiscence discussion. Leave scope for people who do not say much to join in singing the big theme tunes. They might also enjoy listening to others repeating famous sayings and catch-phrases from popular films.

● If you can show some clips from popular old films on video, you can often help people to remember who they went to see that film with and where. It is surprising how vividly people remember the stories of certain films and also the gossip and scandal associated with the stars.

● You might even make a scrap book of the group's favourite stars, which will certainly be a remembered activity for many.

File note extracts of the joint meeting 14/7/98 taken by Hannah Zielig, Observer, London
Theme: What we did to entertain ourselves.
Creative method: Dramatic improvisation and music

The session began quite informally, as people arranged themselves at tables and talked about what they had done in the last week.

It had been decided that the main subject for the session would be the cinema. We would try to incorporate everyone's memories of their youth, when they used to go to the 'pictures'. One of the volunteers, Lil, had brought with her scrapbooks of filmstars that she had kept when she was a teenager. There was a preliminary, general conversation about some of the memories which people had shared last week including:

● watching talent contests before the film started
● queuing up for the cinema
● singing the 'Minors of the ABC' Cinema song,
● hearing the organ before the film started

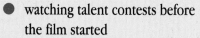
May, aged 97, in action (London)

Everyone then split up into groups to choose somebody's memory and work out how to act it out for everyone else. Before any of the scenes were shown, there was a great deal of practising and lively chat. This resulted in an atmosphere of hilarity and good humour, which infected everyone present. I decided to observe the practising rather than to take part in any of the shows.

Each group was careful to integrate people with dementia equally with others, and to find them a role in the scene which was explained to them fully. There was a real sense of working together and partnership, as everyone was engaged in the proceedings. After approximately fifteen minutes, Pam asked people to perform their pieces to one another. There was surprisingly little embarrassment as carers, carees and volunteers got ready to act in front of others. This is partly due to the sense of trust that has been built up in the whole group. Nobody felt that they would be ridiculed and everyone was prepared to trust that their contribution would be well received.

In one group, May, aged 97, was the mother who had to give her daughters money for the cinema. Contrary to expectations, May refused to give the pennies over saying they 'd already had money for sweets. This had not been rehearsed earlier and the others in the group had to develop their improvised argument with Mum. After much persuasion, the money was handed over. May's surprise change of plan delighted everyone, May included, and the group went along with her idea.

Pam then organised everyone to stand in a cinema queue with Ted in role as a commissionaire. People sang the cinema song as they queued and jostled and then went to sit down as if watching a film. Olive played different styles of music which might have accompanied various films - people reacted spontaneously to the music as if they were watching films.
When Olive played lively music, people banged their feet in time and shouted out, when sad music was played people went quietly and pretended to cry. Violet hassled people around her, in a realistic rendition of what she used to be like during films.

There followed a break for tea and whilst eating and drinking everyone was asked to reminisce about their favourite moments in the cinema, the **'magic moments'** which they had enjoyed.

People then acted out various scenes from the films that they had enjoyed: Ian borrowed Edith's stick in order to mime a scene from a James Mason film **'The Seventh Veil'**, Lil, Eileen and Joyce together sang **'Sonny Boy'** which many people joined in with a rendition of Al Jolson. Ralph acted out a man balancing on a tall building - a Buster Keaton silent movie. Pat Milner sang **'Whip Crack Away'** from the Doris Day film **'Calamity Jane'**.

Most of the scenes were immediately recognised by the audience and a state of excitement was palpable amongst everyone. A whole group of volunteers, workers and carers led by Pam joined in a lively spontaneous rendition of Dorothy, Tin Man, Cowardly Lion etc walking up the yellow brick road in **'The Wizard of Oz'** and all the 'audience' sang or whistled along.

The session concluded with a rendition of 'If I had a talking picture of you', a popular song from the 1930s which the group had jointly remembered the previous week.

'DANCING THE NIGHT AWAY'
LISTENING TO MUSIC AND DANCING

- Talk about where members used to go out to dance halls, church halls, assembly rooms. What did people wear and who did they go with? How did they learn to dance? How did they find a suitable partner?

- Talk about first boyfriends and girlfriends. This is a good opportunity to play popular dance music of that era and invite those who want to to dance. Many people will be happy just to watch and remember quietly their own dancing days.

- People who do not find talking easy often remember the words of songs and will enjoy singing along when the old classics are played. Others will whistle or just nod to the music and find pleasure in just listening while others dance.

CLOSING ACTIVITIES

- Play some dance music, to listen to or to dance to, perhaps 'The Last Waltz'.

Edith enjoys drawing an old gramophone while she and Hannah compare notes on their favourite music. (London)

ACTIVITIES TO TRY OUTSIDE THE GROUP

- Look for photos of the person with dementia when they were young and dressed up to go to a special event. Take time to look at the clothes and hairstyle and shoes and see if any memories remain about that time. The dress may have been specially made by hand, perhaps by someone in the family or the person themselves when young. If the clothes were bought, are there any recollections connected with the important fashion shops of the time. If the shop, or the street where it was, is still there, take a trip to have a look at the area and see what memories come back.

- Find out if there is a local group or centre offering 'tea-dances'. Go along to watch and listen, or participate. Think about places the person with dementia used to go when they were young. If these are local, plan a trip to revisit them, perhaps with a friend from that time.

- Go to the library and look for books of photographs of local cinemas or dance halls.

- Take the person with dementia on a special outing back to somewhere where they used to enjoy themselves when young.

- Look for old records or tapes of familiar and favourite songs or music and set aside a little time each week to play and enjoy them again.

"Yesterday I looked with Mother at old photographs of her when she was 18 or 19 years old. I really had to ask questions as I wanted to learn about what they showed and she still was able to tell me about them, to explain. It was a lovely feeling for Mother as well as for me. "

Carer, Leuven

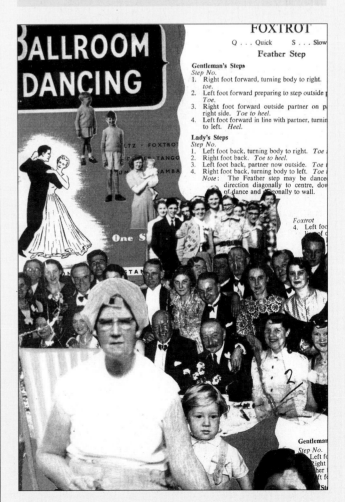

A collage made on a particular theme which was important in a person's life. (Karen Jarvis, Hull, UK)

COURTSHIP AND MARRIAGE

This theme is often a very enjoyable one, taking people back to a special day in their lives. They can rediscover the feelings they had and remember happy times they had with the person they married. However, some group members may never have married, while others may be on second marriages, so that for some people the topic needs to be widened to general memories of romance. Partnerships without marriage can be talked about, and these can include same sex relationships, which might be described as close friendships.

For some members who may have recently lost a partner this may also be a painful subject. However if the group is well-established and supportive, talking about a loss, and sharing memories about the time spent with the person who has died can be helpful and even enjoyable. This theme leads on naturally to discussion about setting up one's first home, the early days of married life and the arrival of the first child. It is important for leaders to have information regarding loss of children or childless marriages, so that they can deal sensitively with participants' feelings.

The theme may also be linked to others such as *'Dressing up and looking good'*, *'Special days and festivals'* and *'Wartime Memories'*.

TRIGGERS

Love letters, jewellery, marriage certificates, wedding photographs, wedding dress, bills for reception, flowers, wedding presents people have kept.

STARTERS

- Sing some songs connected with courtship and marriage - *'Daisy, Daisy'*, *'I'm getting married in the morning'* and the *'Why am I always the bridesmaid, never the blushing bride?'* song.

- Ask all members to bring a photograph of a wedding, their own or another, and begin by arranging them in order of date. Leaders and helpers can bring their photos too. This gives the opportunity to compare notes on fashions and styles at different times.

"*One of the couples began to talk about how they first met up. They danced to a well known hit tune, which now they only remembered the title of. Several of the others in the group, relatives and people with dementia, began to hum the song and ended singing the entire text. It was a sweet song about love and they sang it entirely from memory. It was an emotional moment.*"

Stockholm

The photo of his wedding day was enlarged for Dennis and he then remembered about the tie he was wearing. "A bit loud, some people thought", was his comment, and he remembered the colours. His wife was astonished that he had remembered this and spoken about it to a volunteer as he normally spoke very little. (London)

A wedding photo with a preserved bouquet and the original dress material is recorded at the session so that the participant can refer back to the wedding and the reminiscence session relating to it. (Stockholm)

People often keep many mementos of their wedding day and honeymoon, so ask members to bring along any objects or records of their own or family weddings, including wedding clothes, records of the reception such as the menu or the bill if they have kept these, photos of them cutting the cake, bridesmaids dresses, a bill for the ring, or the ring itself. Pass them round saying briefly something about the memories they evoke.

ACTIVITIES

'THE MONKEY PARADE'
ACTING OUT

Talk about where members used to go to meet other young people. How did it feel when you were young? Perhaps enact what you used to do, for example walking up and down with a best friend and seeing if there was anyone you liked the look of. Comparing notes on flirting strategies can be funny and might interest both sexes.

'BACK BY TEN'
ACTING OUT

Talk about going out, time to be in by, what happened if you were late, boyfriends or girlfriends being brought home for the first time. Act out some of these memories in small groups with one person playing Mother, another Father and two playing the courting couple.

'THE BOTTOM DRAWER'
LISTING AND USING OBJECTS

The trousseau: what did people put in their bottom drawers and how did they pay for it? What was considered necessary to accumulate before getting married? This could include dowries and particular requirements in minority religious and cultural groups.

Make a case or drawer with a few sheets and tablecloths in. Ask people to make suggestions as to what they would like to put in it. Assemble all these things (or as many as possible or their modern equivalents)

'FIRST HOME'
DISCUSSION AND WRITING

In small groups discuss how people saved for their weddings, how long were they engaged, where they first lived when they were married (for example with in-laws) and their plans for a home of their own. Talk about and write down what you took to your first home, what basic furniture you had and where it came from.

'THE WEDDING LIST'
LISTING AND DRAWING

In small groups discuss the wedding presents received. Make a list of them and read them out to the other groups, so that more memories are triggered. Notice the differences during wartime periods. Make a drawing of some of the wedding presents.

Some people had wedding present lists which were sent out to guests and they may have kept a copy or be able to recall some of the items on it when *'jogged'* by other people's lists. If people have kept any of their wedding presents ask them to bring them in to show.

'A WEDDING GROUP'
COLLAGE

Ask members to bring in wedding photographs, then photocopy and enlarge these to share and enjoy at the next meeting. A group collage of all the images could then be made.

'OLD UNCLE TOM COBLEY'
ACTING OUT

In small groups talk about wedding receptions, who came, where were they held, wedding food, music played. Had the couple's families met before and how did they get along? Include traumas recalled from weddings (for example people getting drunk, not turning up, forgetting speeches, catering disasters, wedding cars not arriving, wine or beer all being drunk before).

Pick one of the stories and act them out for the whole group.

Two group leaders dress up in wedding clothes to help the group remember their own weddings. (Stockholm)

'SOMETHING BORROWED, SOMETHING BLUE' DISCUSSION

- Wedding traditions are different from one region to another and in different cultures; something blue to be worn, tin cans attached to cars, confetti, rice, throwing bouquets.

- Share stories about different ways of celebrating which members of the group have been involved in or seen in other parts of the world.

'WARTIME WEDDINGS' SHARING STORIES IN THE GROUP

- Getting round ration restrictions, black market goods, preparing a wedding dress at short notice from whatever material could be found, sharing dresses with other brides, pooling rations for wedding reception food, getting married quickly because the fiancee was going to be sent abroad.

'WATCH THE BIRDIE' TABLEAU

- Make a wedding group using the people in the group as bride and groom, bridesmaids, mother in law, unwelcome guests. If you have a camera, take a photograph of it. If not, take an imaginary photo, getting everyone to 'freeze'.

'HONEYMOONS' FANTASY JOURNEY

- Going away outfits, journeys, destinations, secret honeymoons. Try a guided fantasy about an ideal honeymoon with an imaginary partner, such as Clark Gable. Where would you go? What would you do? Bring some travel brochures for members to choose an ideal destination.

CLOSING ACTIVITIES

- Invite members of the group to make a short vote of thanks to their husband or wife (whether alive or dead). You could also ask people to recall a real vote of thanks which was given at their own wedding.

- Play a recording of the wedding march on tape, choose somebody to be the bride and groom and lead the way out of the session.

ACTIVITIES OUTSIDE THE GROUP

- Take the person on a visit to the church, synagogue or registry office where they got married. Have a look at the register and see if you can find a mention of their wedding.

- Take out old photo albums including wedding photos and look at them with the person with dementia. It is a good idea to write on the back of the photo the names of the people, so that if they are not remembered, you can turn the photo over and discover together who they are.

Diane Heine, group leader enjoys being a 'blushing bride' in a session on Wedding Days. (Kassel)

- Make contact with someone who came to the wedding and ask them to share their memories, either by coming round or by writing a letter. Set some time aside at home to talk over the very special moments from courting days. This must not become a test of memory, as failure could be upsetting for both parties. It is more helpful if the carer talks about his or her own memories and allows the person with dementia to add in memories or phrases spontaneously if these are triggered.

> **One carer told how he and his wife had spoken about their first canoeing trip together, "how much they were in love, and how they had tied up the canoe in the reeds". The carer said that this was the first conversation in years between him and his wife where they were on the same wavelength.**
>
> **Amsterdam**

OUTINGS AND HOLIDAYS

Many older people may have memories of day trips rather than holidays, so make sure that local days out are included when talking about holidays. Some older people will have had their first real holiday as young adults. Topics to explore might include staying in 'bed and breakfasts' and hotels, going abroad for the first time, Sunday School outings, works outings, train or coach journeys, bicycle rides and picnics.

TRIGGERS

Tapes of seaside sounds and bird calls, picture postcards, photographs (personal and general) of holiday places including holidays abroad pictures of old cars and caravans, rucksack, camping equipment, bucket and spade, panama hats or straw boaters, picnic hamper, flask, bathing suits and caps, shells, souvenirs, pen-knife, sticks of rock, handkerchief tied at four corners

STARTERS

● Sing a song which reminds people of holidays for example *'Oh, I do like to be beside the seaside', 'My knapsack on my back'.*

● Ask the group to relax, close their eyes and listen to a tape of the sound of waves breaking on a beach and seagulls crying. After a few minutes, go into pairs or small groups and talk about what the sounds remind them of.

Maria remembers a holiday in Yugoslavia and demonstrates how she danced to music from that country. (Amsterdam)

● Pass round a bucket or a basket and invite everyone to put in something which they would like to take with them on a holiday or an outing. This could be items of food for a picnic or sweets to eat on the way or a swimming suit, bucket and spade, pullover or hat. Accept whatever people offer and enjoy the suggestions, however bizarre.

Friends having a paddle, circa 1930 (London)

ACTIVITIES

'THE FIRST TIME....'
SMALL GROUP DISCUSSION

- Explore memories of early holidays and day trips, including the first time people went away or saw the sea or the countryside. Prompts might include seaside entertainment, donkey rides, Punch and Judy shows, beach sports, fairground rides, special seaside food. For the countryside, prompts might include picnic menus, bicycle rides, rare birds spotted, paddling and swimming in rivers, seeing farm animals for the first time.

"If the person with dementia can no longer easily articulate memories the carer might tell a holiday story to the group or a volunteer, including the person with dementia in the conversation as they tell the story. 'We had lovely holidays in Rhyl didn't we? Do you remember that first time, just after we were married when we stayed in that bed and breakfast. This is a photograph of us both on the sea front. We were only young then.'"

'READY FOR OFF'
OBJECTS TO PACK AND HANDLE

- Bring an old-fashioned leather suitcase and fill it with holiday things y, such as old pyjamas, 'long johns' and 'combinations', socks, a nice dress, tis sue paper for careful packing, a stiff collar for an evening out, binoculars, a swim suit, straw hats, blow-up beach ball, shaving set, jelly shoes, old money, and possibly an old passport.

- Unpack the suitcase with the group and talk about the contents. Invite suggestions for things to be packed. Repack the suitcase and close it. Tie string around it and remind people about sitting on suitcases to close them when they were too full. Some people may remember their suitcases being collected from home by a carter and taken by train to the destination. Then imagine someone who might have packed this suitcase. On the basis of what is in it, make up a story about the person who owned it, where they were going, who with and for what purpose. What happened on the journey and why was the suitcase abandoned? It can be very enjoyable to make a fantasy history for an object in this way as a group and all contributions to the story should be accepted, however far-fetched.

'A PICTURE POSTCARD'
DRAWING AND WRITING

- Use the memories emerging from the small groups to plan a picture to be drawn from the person's memories by them or a helper. Use plenty of colours and let the choice of colour be determined by the person remembering. If a helper is doing the drawing on behalf of a person with dementia, they should constantly check back to see if they are imagining it right. On the back of the picture (or beside it on another piece of paper) write a message about the remembered holiday, and decide who to address it to.

An improvisation using seaside objects drawing on memories of earlier times. (London)

Everyone is doing seaside activities and playing games together in the imaginary photo taken by Jim on his Box Brownie camera. (London)

'SNAPSHOT DRAMAS'
ACTING OUT

● Following discussion in small groups, ask each group to choose a memory of a holiday or day trip and act it out. Choose a story with characters and action or just a single moment remembered, like licking a huge ice cream or getting in a muddle with a deck chair or trying to get in or out of a swimming costume on a crowded beach.

"If leaders and members have information about where people used to go on holiday or who they went with, they can act as 'extra memory' for the person with dementia. Names can be put to places and people to help bring back memories for the person with dementia. Appropriate triggers, for example photos or maps of places that were visited, can also be brought to the meeting, to help stimulate memories."

'MAPPING THE ROUTE'
NAMING THINGS AND PLACES

● If you can find out from relatives or carers where people went on holiday you can look at the route and retrace these familiar journeys using old road and railway maps and saying the names of the places passed through on the journey. People may remember places where they stopped for refreshments or times when the transport broke down and will have associated memories. The same can be done with cycle rides or places where people went on rambles in the countryside. The representation of the journey in an old map or guide serves to help people relocate themselves in that time.

"A carer reminded his wife about a time when she had driven a car through the Russian occupied zone of Germany to Berlin. She then was able to tell the story in great detail to a volunteer enjoying the memory of how independent she had felt and how much courage it had needed for a young woman to do this. Although it was the carer who provided the initial trigger, the exciting thing for her was to tell the story to a new listener."

Kassel

'I CAN HEAR IT NOW....'
SOUND COLLAGE

● Make your own sound collage in the group, after some discussion about the kinds of sounds you might hear. These might include the sound of a candy floss seller, brass bands, sea gulls, or mountain streams, horses' hooves, train whistles and country sounds.

'HALF A CROWN TO BRIGHTON'
IMAGINARY JOURNEY

● Talk about day trips as a child by charabanc, train or steamer. Talk about what people might have taken with them and who they might have gone with. Retrace the journey in action, reorganising the furniture to help people to imagine they are really travelling somewhere in a train a coach, a car or a boat. Look over the side of the imaginary boat or through the train or coach window, pointing out what you are seeing. Ask everyone to help build up a group picture of the journey, calling out new sights.

'THE BEANO'
STORY TELLING PROMPTED BY A PHOTO

● Often pubs or work places had an annual outing and for many older people this was the only holiday they had. Memories associated with these outings might include what people wore, how drunk people got, office or factory hierarchies breaking down and people misbehaving themselves.

● Try to find a photo of such an outing, with everyone in their best clothes on the charabanc and see what associations this has for members of the group.

'WORKING HOLIDAYS'
SHOWING THE ACTIONS

● For some women and children, the seasonal work available in the countryside provided an opportunity for a working holiday. Many people have fond memories of hop-picking, apple picking, and other country activities which involved them in staying somewhere different, often in spartan conditions, including sleeping in cattle sheds or tents.

● Have a go at demonstrating how hops or other crops were picked. If they remember a song associated with the work, sing it as a group.

● Discuss how people spent the money earned on these working holidays.

'SEASIDE SENSATIONS'
SENSORY STIMULATION

● Bring some sand or shells in for people to enjoy. The feel of sand running through fingers (or even between the toes), the sound of the sea in a sea shell or the feel and smell of slimy seaweed can evoke powerful memories. Although some people may not be able to articulate their memories, the introduction of physical activities helps to transport them back to remembered pleasures.

"When we go down hopping...." - a working holiday in Kent - hard work but rules were relaxed, children stayed up late and Booth's gin was drunk by parents in the evenings. (London)

The feel and smell of a rubber swimming cap or the roughness of a woollen swimming costume can help to make the picture more complete. Bringing in real ice creams in cones or wafers may be the most powerful way for some people to remember the tastes associated with the seaside.

'BRIC A BRAC'
AN ARRANGEMENT OF MEMORABILIA

Ask carers to bring in souvenirs from holidays. They might collect objects, photos and postcards and arrange them during the session with a volunteer who might hear the memories behind the things brought in. A photograph could then be taken of the carer and the person with dementia with their 'holiday collection' or a group collection of holiday ephemera could be mounted.

'THE HOLIDAY OF A LIFETIME'
DRAWING, COLLAGE, WRITING

Draw a picture, or make a collage in pairs using images from travel brochures of somewhere you would like to go on holiday, or the best holiday you ever had. If this is just a fantasy, decide who you would like to take with you (it could be a famous person, film star or favourite crooner) and what you would do and talk about. Send an imaginary postcard back from this holiday.

A family carer has made a holiday collage. (Vienna)

A collage of holiday images and objects (Stockholm)

CLOSING ACTIVITIES

Have a sing-song of all the songs people remember singing on the way home in the bus or car. Choose popular numbers and just do the choruses of two or three, such as *'Show me the way to go home'* or *'My bonnie lies over the ocean'*. Take an imaginary (or real) photo of the group as though you have just been on an outing. For this it is fun to have sun hats or panamas to wear, buckets and spades to hold up or an old rucksack to carry on one's back.

ACTIVITIES OUTSIDE THE GROUP

Revisit somewhere the person with dementia used to go to - take a day trip to the seaside for instance, perhaps with a grandchild, telling them stories of past outings.

Select some holiday photographs and put them into a frame to enjoy

"We looked at old pictures and visited friends who triggered memories. Last summer we stayed at the farm like in the olden days. He loved the farming memories."

Oslo

Go to the library and see if you can find photographs or books about places you and the person with dementia have enjoyed visiting, or ask a friend or member of the family to look for you.

Watch a slide show or cine film of past holidays sharing your memories and seeing whether they trigger memories for the person with dementia.

Avoid testing the person with dementia - they may not remember anything, but if you share your memories, these may act as triggers for the person with dementia.

SPECIAL DAYS AND FESTIVALS

This topic is about festivals and celebrations, and customs. What people celebrate will vary depending on their age, religion and culture, so leaders must find out from their group members which dates and customs are important to them. However you approach it, the topic offers the chance to make the room and atmosphere special, to dress up and enjoy special food associated with a particular day or festival. Although you may have a meeting where 'Special Days and Festivals' is the specified topic, anniversaries, birthdays and seasonal festivals will occur throughout the life of a group and can be enjoyed as they happen from week to week.

TRIGGERS

(There will be national, regional, cultural and individual differences.)

Easter chicks, eggs, hot cross buns, Christmas decorations, Palm Sunday crosses, harvest festival wheats and grasses, Passover plates and Chanukka candles, prayer mat, Divali lights, Eid cards, Chinese dragons, coronation mugs, souvenirs, newspapers reporting world events, flags, kites

Group leaders sent out a letter in advance asking people how they celebrated Easter so that they were well prepared for the topic. Different customs remembered included Easter witches, putting sweets or money in the coffee pot, Easter kisses, putting twigs into vases of water and decorating them with feathers. (Stockholm)

"For the Easter meeting, I brought a cock made out of porcelain to our session and on the table there was the cock plus boiled eggs. We painted the eggs in different colours and then we brought them home with us. We had "Konacke" bread, and candy out of Easter eggs, delicious! We like to remember all the Easter evenings we've spent at the country house, first with the children, then with their 'companions' whom they eventually married, and later with the grandchildren. We ate the same traditional foods throughout the years. These traditions are important, especially now when Stig has difficulties with his memory. We have a lot of things in common to talk about, arising out of discussions on the project."

Carer's Diary, Stockholm

STARTERS

Sing a Christmas song - *'Jingle bells'*, *'I'm dreaming of a white Christmas'* - or a birthday song - or a hymn appropriate to the season, for example, *'We plough the fields and scatter the good seed on the land'* at harvest time.

A carefully arranged table and candles create a warm atmosphere for sharing photos and memories of earlier special times. (Kassel)

ACTIVITIES

'MANY HAPPY RETURNS'
DANCING AND EXCHANGING GIFTS

- Encourage group members to share birthdays and anniversaries with the group. This can provide group meetings with a special atmosphere and give the group a feeling of closeness and an excuse to have fun. Carers may bring in a cake and leaders or helpers can provide food and drink. Giving cards and little presents can take people back to other special occasions. Putting flowers on the table or presenting special floral button holes can create a festive atmosphere in which everyone's spirits are lifted.

"When Jim and Joan danced the Anniversary Waltz and we all sang, I had tears in my eyes. Everyone felt moved by the occasion."

Volunteer, London

'DEAR SANTA CLAUS'
DRAWING/PAINTING/WRITING

- In pairs or small groups, talk about a present you had or would like to have had as a child for Christmas or a birthday. As a group write down some of the presents people remember asking Santa to bring, and share memories of writing to him as children. Then draw a picture (with one person telling and the other drawing) of one particular present remembered. Share the pictures and the stories with the whole group at the end of the session.

'PARTY PIECES'
SONGS AND RECITATION

- Maybe some people remember family parties at Christmas or other festivals where everyone had their party piece or favourite recitation. If anyone in the group remembers a song or poem they were always asked to perform, ask them to run through it now, with help from the rest of the group who are likely to remember similar 'turns'.

- Some people may even remember the actions they had to do with these numbers. Carers can help the group leader by thinking beforehand about what songs and poems might 'ring a bell' and bring them along with the words written out to help if necessary.

'TRICK OR TREAT'
ACTING OUT OR WRITING DOWN

- Talk about customs when you were young, such as those involving *'naughty'* behaviour which was allowed on a special day (for example, letting off bangers on fire-work night, *'knocking down ginger'*, *'trick or treat'*, student *'rag weeks'*, *'stag nights'* before a wedding, Hogmanay binges). Other customs might include embarrassing school rituals for new pupils or initiation pranks for new apprentice workers. If there's a good story in your group act it out or write it down for the rest of the group to enjoy.

'ALL THINGS NICE'
FOOD MAKING AND TASTING

- The taste and smell of food can be very evocative. When planning, if carers and people with dementia can be involved, favourite recipes or dishes could be prepared at home and brought to the meeting to share with other members.

- Alternatively, if there are adequate facilities, preparing and cooking together could be a really enjoyable group activity. On Pancake Day, for instance, pancakes could be made and eaten together at the meeting.

Handling old cooking implements used in preparing festive food. (Leuven)

- If you are cooking, make sure that people with dementia participate in a way which minimises the risk of failure. For instance, have everyone share mixing ingredients, but then have the leader make them and take the risk of dropping the mixture or not managing to flip the pancakes very expertly.

- Other ideas for cooking and eating are foods associated with childhood days, such as fairy cakes or jellies in exciting shapes using jelly mould. Many people associate particular foods with events in the religious calendar, such as hot cross buns for Easter, mince pies for Christmas, cinnamon cakes for Passover.

- Share ideas of special recipes, then write them down and make them into a little booklet with entries under different festivals, seasons and occasions. Some older people will remember recipes involving parts of animals which we no longer eat and it is enjoyable and amusing to remember how Mother made brawn or cooked sheep's ears or made rook or pigeon pie.

'RITES OF PASSAGE'
RELIGIOUS FESTIVALS & OBSERVANCES

- For many older people, religious customs and festivals formed an important part of early life. There were also social activities connected with churches or other places of worship. Milestones in a person's life may have been marked with a religious ceremony, for instance Bar Mizvah or Confirmation.

A young girl ready for her confirmation, 1931 (Copenhagen)

A boy posing for his Bar Mizvah photograph in the 1920's (London)

- Some customs may no longer be practised or known about by leaders and younger members, so opportunities need to be given for carers or others to help introduce memories of significant rituals practised in the past. Leaders might find information to help jog memories in the local library. A local church or community organisation may be able to provide appropriate books or images.

- Objects, such as prayer shawls, rosaries, veils and prayer books, can help people to remember or can just be passed around the group and enjoyed for their texture and feel. People may well want to enact the rituals they remember, such as making a religious obeisance or singing responses or prayers.

'SUNDAY BEST'
TALKING AND DRAWING

- Sunday (or whatever was the Sabbath day) was markedly different from other days in the week. As it was the only day off, families often spent time together, saw relatives, wore special clothes, ate special food, went to church or Sunday school (sometimes several times in a day). In many families, there were things you were not allowed to do on the Sabbath and this caused considerable irritation for young people. People may also remember the street sellers who came round, especially on a Sunday, offering cockles and whelks for Sunday tea or muffins on a tray (advertised by ringing a bell). Ask the group what they remember about childhood Sundays. Draw a picture of them or their parents in their Sunday best.

"The group were reminiscing about the Coronation of Elizabeth II in 1953. People swapped stories about where they spent Coronation Day. One carer remembered that she had been helping her mum in the pub which she ran and that they had been particularly busy that day. As she sketched in the story of how the Irish family next door brought round their tin bath and asked to have it filled up with beer, her mother (aged 97) who had not remembered anything about the day until that point, suddenly nodded and brightened up. She then spontaneously volunteered "There was a fight. A big fight. There was a stabbing. This man was all packed out with bandages. Taken to hospital." The daughter was reminded of this by her mother and everyone was enthralled by the whole story as told by the pair of them."

London

'WHERE WERE YOU WHEN...?'
A SHARING EXPERIENCE

● Ask the group to think about memorable and historic dates which have occurred during their lifetime. Where were they when these events occurred? This is a way of bringing the group together and locating them again in their earlier lives at that particular time. Topics like the death or coronation of a ruling monarch, or the outbreak of war and its ending are possible subjects. Relatively recent events such as the assassination of President Kennedy or the moon landing can also trigger memories.

● The people with dementia may not remember anything when the topic is first mentioned, but will often find that when the time is sketched in by a family member or another member of the group, they do recognise and remember that time. Pictures of the event will help and even film footage on video, if this is available. Even if individual members have no memories of that time, they can still enjoy the memories of the rest of the group and some may even find that they can add to the stories being told after all, once their memory has been jogged and they are enjoying being *'back in those times'*.

'OUR OWN GROUP SCRAPBOOK'
RECORDING THE GROUP

● Take photographs of the group enjoying celebrating and make copies for group members to take home and enjoy later. A polaroid camera is particularly good because it allows members to see themselves recorded instantly in a number of different poses. Photographs can also be copied and enlarged to be enjoyed in future meetings. They can be taken home and used by the carer to help the person with dementia remember what they were doing, and the enjoyment they had in the group.

CLOSING ACTIVITIES

● Sing Auld Lang Syne or other well-known ending song.

ACTIVITIES OUTSIDE THE GROUP

● When a special day is coming up, for instance Easter or Christmas, spend some time reminding the person with dementia about how the day used to be spent in the past. Go to the library and see if there are books about the topic. Share them without testing the person with dementia, and see what, if anything, triggers memories.

In the last meeting before Christmas, a woman who knew how to play the recorder walked round the room and played all the Christmas tunes and carols requested by the group. (Kassel)

Bibliography

Reminiscence

Reminiscence Reviewed
Ed. Joanna Bornat, Open University Press, 1995

Reminiscence and Recall
Faith Gibson, Age Concern,. 1998

Reminiscence Activities
Roger Sim, Winslow Press, 1998

Reminiscence in Dementia Care
Ed. Pam Schweitzer, Age Exchange, 1998

The Meaning of Reminiscence and Life Review
Ed. Jon Hendricks, Baywood, 1995

Narrative Identity and Dementia
Marie Mills, Aldershot, 1998

The Reminiscence Handbook
Caroline Osborn, Age Exchange, 1993

Dementia

Care Assistant's Guide to working with People with Dementia,
Ed. Sue Benson, Journal of Dementia Care, 1994

The Carer's Companion
Richard Corney, Winslow Press, 1994

Alzheimers - A Practical Guide for Carers to Help You Through the Day
Frena Gray Davidson, Piatkus Books, 1993

The Long and Winding Road
Jane Gilliard, Wrightson Biomedical, 1995

Dementia Reconsidered,
Tom Kitwood, Open University Press, 1997

Personal Experience & Biography

My Journey into Alzheimers
R. Davis, Scripture Press, 1989

Remind Me Who I Am, Again
Linda Grant, Bloomsbury Press, 1998

Iris Murdoch, a Memoir
John Bayley, Abacus, 1998

Living in the Labyrinth
Diana Friel McGowin, Elder Books, 1993

You are Words, Dementia Poems
Edited and introduced by John Killick,
Journal of Dementia Care, 1997

Always Alice
Ted Cunningham, Equal Arts, 1995

Caring for Maria
Bernard Heywood, Element Books, 1994

Novels

Have the Men Had Enough?
Margaret Forster, Penguin Books, 1989

Scar Tissue
Michael Ignatieff, Chatto & Windus, 1993

Memory
Margaret Mahy, Penguin books, 1989

Memory Board
Janet Rule, Pandora, 1987

Gertie Marshall teaches Pam Schweitzer a song from long ago. (London)